Massachusetts

Massachusetts

Sylvia McNair

Children's Press®
A Division of Grolier Publishing
New York London Hong Kong Sydney
Danbury, Connecticut

This book is dedicated to the several members of my family who received degrees from fine Massachusetts schools— Boston University, Massachusetts Institute of Technology, Radcliffe College, and Simmons College.

**Frontispiece: An aerial view of Boston's wharf
and financial district
Front cover: Beacon Hill, Boston, in autumn
Back cover: A cranberry bog**

Consultants: Brenda Howitson and Mary B. Bicknell, Massachusetts State Library

Please note: All statistics are as up-to-date as possible at the time of publication.

Visit Children's Press on the Internet at http://publishing.grolier.com

Book production by Editorial Directions, Inc.

Library of Congress Cataloging-in-Publication Data

McNair, Sylvia.
    Massachusetts / by Sylvia McNair.
        p. cm. — (America the beautiful. Second series)
    Includes bibliographical references (p.) and index.
    Summary: Describes the history, geography, ecology, people, economy,
cities, and sights of the Bay State, Massachusetts.
    ISBN 0-516-20635-4
    1. Massachusetts—Juvenile literature. [1. Massachusetts.] I. Title. II. Series.
F64.3.M44 1998
974.4—dc21   97-40668
                                                                                  CIP
                                                                                   AC

Acknowledgments

The author is grateful for the assistance of many people in Massachusetts, including personnel at Boston Public Library, the Massachusetts Office of Tourism, and the Regional Tourist Councils. They supplied great quantities of important and interesting materials—far more than it was possible to include in this book.

Plimouth Plantation

Cape Cod

The First Thanksgiving

Ted Williams

Contents

Crab fisher

Sugar maples and ash

Cranberry harvesting

Ladybug

One Day in 1627

I t is a beautiful summer day. Elizabeth Hopkins is pulling a few weeds from her kitchen garden. She is daydreaming, remembering her childhood in England.

"Oh dear, my new herb plants are still too small for picking," she sighs. "My pottage really needs something to add a little flavor and make it smell delicious." Elizabeth has been working all morning, preparing a stew for dinner. She gathered vegetables from the garden, peeled them, chopped them, and added a few pieces of leftover meat.

Interpreters in period clothing re-create life in 1627 at Plimoth Plantation.

"Maybe Bridget Fuller will let me have a few sprigs of thyme or marjoram," she thinks. The Fullers' home is only two doors away.

There are only a few homes in the village of Plimoth. Each one is on a fenced-in lot, and all of them have gardens. The houses are small and simple. The men of the village have built them all. They cut the trees, shaped the trunks into house timbers, and made the pieces needed to frame the building. They also built a meeting-house, storehouses, barns for hay, and shelters for animals.

Opposite: The *Mayflower II*

A new home is under construction now, and soon all the men of the village will get together to raise the frame. Then the steep, sloping roof will be covered with thatch to keep out the rain and snow.

A group of schoolchildren from a nearby town will be visiting the village today. Elizabeth will welcome them, show them her home, tell them all about her daily chores, and answer their questions. Other villagers will talk with them, too.

Plimoth Plantation is a re-creation of the village settled by a small colony of English people who sailed to Massachusetts in

Plimoth Plantation

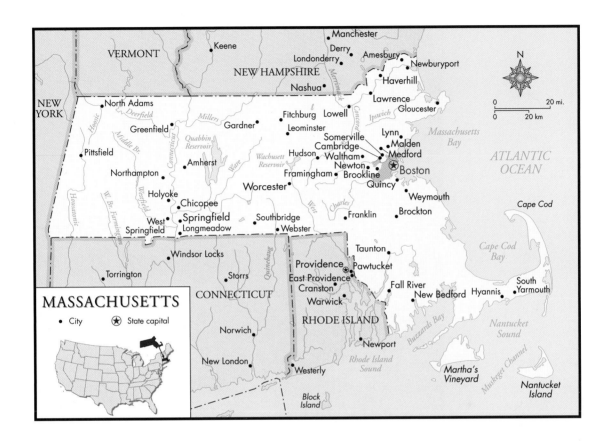

Geopolitical map of Massachusetts

1620. People in period costume act out daily life as it was then and talk to visitors as if it were actually a day in 1627. They speak only about things known to the early settlers—they've never heard of electric lights, airplanes, or television. They wear the clothes people wore then, use the tools used then, and prepare the kind of food early settlers found or grew for themselves.

The villagers, called interpreters, haven't even heard of the United States. There was no United States in 1627, and there would not be for another 150 years. They live in the Plimoth (or Plymouth) Colony of North America.

Legend says Plymouth Rock was the spot where the Pilgrims first stepped into the New World.

After spending several hours in the village, the visiting children can stop in at Hobbamock's Homesite. Hobbamock was a real person, a member of the Wampanoag people, who lived for a while with the colonists. Interpreters explain what life was like for the Native Americans who lived there. They demonstrate such skills as weaving and building a dugout canoe.

The last adventure of the day is to board *Mayflower II,* a reproduction of the small ship that brought the Pilgrims to New England. Visitors can learn about shipbuilding and practice tying knots—something every sailor must know.

On the bus ride home, one of the young visitors comments, "I really feel as if we did visit the colonists at Plymouth and that today actually was a summer day in 1627!"

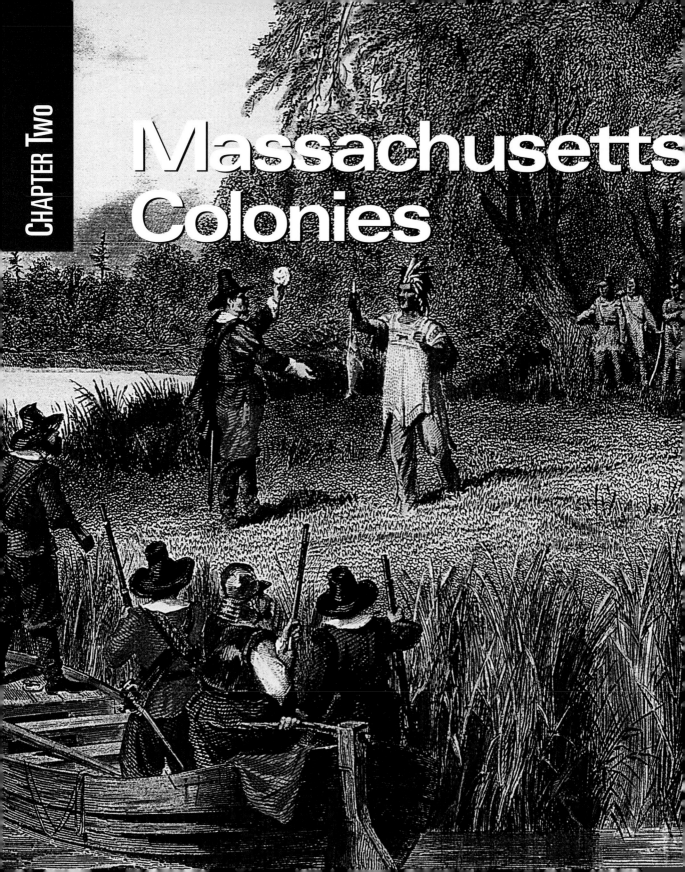

CHAPTER TWO

Massachusetts Colonies

D uring the last Ice Age, great glaciers covered much of North America. When they melted, about 10,000 years ago, small bands of nomadic people came into the region we know as Massachusetts. They found a few huge prehistoric animals—caribou, mammoths, and mastodons. They hunted the animals for meat, used the hides for clothing, and made simple tools from the animals' bones.

Wampanoag interpreters burn a log to make it into a canoe at Plimoth Plantation.

Over the next centuries, the climate continued to warm. Ice and frozen earth gave way to forestlands. Other people arrived. They hunted deer and turkeys, fished for cod, dug for clams, and gathered wild strawberries. They cleared the land and planted corn, beans, and squash.

When the Europeans first came to what is now New England, seven Native American groups were living in the region: the Wampanoag, Nauset, Pennacook, Nipmuc, Pocumtuc, Mohican, and Massachuset.

The Native Americans had a well-organized society and had developed efficient methods and tools for hunting and trapping. They quarried soapstone and carved it into cooking pots. They cut down trees and made dugout canoes of the trunks.

Opposite: An artist's depiction of the Wampanoag greeting the Pilgrims

The Mystery of Dighton Rock

In Dighton Rock State Park, near Fall River, Massachusetts, early colonists discovered a huge 40-ton boulder covered with inscriptions. They assumed the carvings were the work of Native Americans. Later, it was thought that Viking explorers had made them. Still another theory suggests that a sixteenth-century Portuguese explorer may have been responsible. ■

Exploration of Massachusetts

Meat was plentiful, since many mammals roamed the forests. Nuts and wild plants, as well as waterbirds, turtles, and seafood, added variety to the Native American diet.

Early Explorations

Viking explorers from Scandinavia may have been the first Europeans to find their way to the coasts of what are now New England and eastern Canada. During the sixteenth century there were many expeditions across the Atlantic. European nations were interested in the Americas for a variety of reasons. Some hoped to find gold, others wanted valuable furs, and many were drawn by the seemingly endless supplies of fish, which could be preserved in salt and sold in Europe.

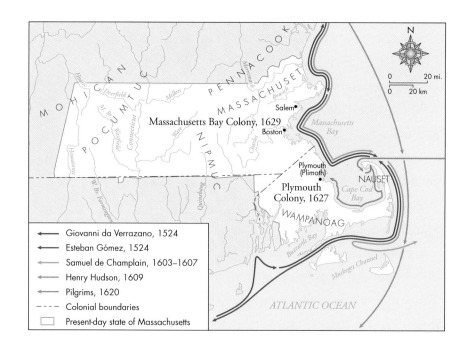

Giovanni da Verrazano, 1524
Esteban Gómez, 1524
Samuel de Champlain, 1603–1607
Henry Hudson, 1609
Pilgrims, 1620
Colonial boundaries
Present-day state of Massachusetts

Place-names

The name *Massachusetts* comes from the Massachuset Indian people. It means "large hill place" or "near the great hill." Many place-names in this state came from Native American words. Some places were named for towns in England, such as Boston, Plymouth, and New Bedford, and a few were named in honor of certain people. For example, Holyoke was named for an early explorer of the Connecticut Valley, and Lowell was named in honor of the man who founded the textile industry in America.

Cape Cod was named by Bartholomew Gosnold, an early English ship captain, for the abundant fish found in the waters around the peninsula. He then sailed farther and landed on a large island covered with grapevines. He named it Martha's Vineyard, for his daughter.

A few years later, Captain John Smith (right) of the Virginia Colony made an expedition to this area. He mapped the coastline and named the area New England. Many present-day place-names appear on that

map. Some are Native American names; others were changed to English names by King Charles I of England. ■

Most people who came to the New World did not plan to stay. They hoped to find treasure of one kind or another and hurry back home. A few saw an opportunity to start a new life, however. One group hoped to find a place where they could worship in their own ways. They disagreed with the way the Church of England was run and wanted to form their own church. They became known as Separatists.

A small group of Separatists first left England for Holland. Later, they joined other emigrants from England and sailed to North America. They were determined to establish a colony based on their own beliefs.

The Mayflower Compact

A small ship, the *Mayflower,* set sail from Plymouth, England, on September 16, 1620. The ship carried too many people and too much cargo—furniture, supplies, and personal possessions. Somehow, that small, overloaded ship made it across the ocean.

On board were thirty-five Separatists and nearly twice as many other passengers and crew. The voyage lasted sixty-five days, and tempers grew short in the crowded conditions.

Before landing, forty-one of the men on the ship held a meeting. They agreed to make their own laws for the new colony and to obey them. The Mayflower Compact was the first document in American history to establish the principle of government by the people and "for the general good" of the people. The original Mayflower Compact no longer exists. It is known only through the text copied by William Bradford into his journals, *Of Plimoth Plantation.*

The Plymouth Colony

The Separatists named their first village Plymouth (or Plimoth), after the English port from which they had sailed. William Bradford, governor of Plymouth Colony for more than twenty years, kept a journal of those early days in the wilderness and later wrote a history of the colony. He called the first colonists "Pilgrims" and described their landing in the New World: "Being thus arrived in a good harbor, and brought safe to land, they fell upon their knees and blessed the God of heaven who had brought them over the vast and furious ocean, again to set their feet on the firm and stable earth."

Only about half the colonists survived that first New England winter. When spring came, the Pilgrims began to plant the seeds they had brought from England.

The Wampanoag who lived in the vicinity left the settlers alone during the winter, but when the weather grew warmer, they

began to visit the newcomers. They shared seeds of native plants and showed the Pilgrims how to use fish as fertilizer for their crops.

After the harvest was gathered in the autumn of 1621, the colonists and the Wampanoag feasted together for three days. They ate venison, several kinds of wild fowl, and vegetables from their gardens. Today, we call that celebration the first Thanksgiving.

The Pilgrim fathers are remembered for their courage in following their own consciences, for signing the Mayflower Compact, and for establishing the first English colony north of Virginia. The colonists had

Who Owned the Land?

Europeans had been traveling to distant lands for several hundred years. They were motivated, all too often, by greed. They wanted land in other parts of the world. Sometimes they accomplished this by trading, many times by warfare and thievery.

The wealthy investors—often kings and queens—who provided the money for these expeditions expected some profit in return. The rulers of Spain, Holland, England (King Charles of England, left), France, and other nations thought native peoples were uncivilized savages and felt that they had a right to exploit such "inferior" creatures. Every explorer wanted to be the first to claim new land by planting the flag of his nation on the new territory.

Native Americans did not think of land as private property. No one claimed to own a piece of land or a stretch of water. Tribes might fight with one another over hunting or fishing rights, but within the tribe everyone shared.

In a few instances, Europeans paid for the land they took from Native Americans, but most Massachusetts colonists believed that the king of England had a right to the land. Therefore, he could give away any of it to individuals or to groups. ▓

to work hard under harsh conditions, but newcomers continued to arrive. By 1627, the Plymouth Colony had become self-sufficient and, by 1630, about 500 English people had settled in the region.

The Massachusetts Bay Colony

Eight years after the Pilgrims landed, some wealthy men in London formed the New England Company to finance another expedition to the region. In 1628, the king gave a grant of land to the company. The land was described as extending from 3 miles (4.8 km) north of the Merrimack River to 3 miles (4.8 km) south of the Charles River and west to the Pacific Ocean. Of course, no one knew then how far away the Pacific was.

In March 1630, ten years after the *Mayflower* landed, the *Arbella* sailed into Massachusetts Bay with 1,000 Puritans on board. John Winthrop, their religious and political leader, was governor of the Massachusetts Bay Colony for more than twenty years.

The Puritans who founded the Massachusetts Bay Colony differed from the Separatists. They didn't want to break away from the Church of England; they just wanted to change the practices they disagreed with. The Puritans came to America because they wanted to worship as they pleased, but within their colony, they expected everyone to follow the Puritan rules whether they were Puritans or not. There was no such thing as separation of church and state and no freedom of worship for non-Puritans.

John Winthrop

An attack on Brookfield during King Philip's War

King Philip's War

For the most part, the colonists and the Native American people of Massachusetts lived peacefully together. The only major conflict between Native Americans and colonists in New England took place in 1675. A Wampanoag chief, called King Philip by the colonists, resented and feared the leaders of the Plymouth Colony. He felt the only way his people could survive was to drive out the settlers. King Philip convinced two other

Religious Persecutions

Some colonists did not believe what the Puritans thought they should, and these disbelievers were dealt with severely. A woman named Anne Hutchinson held meetings in her home to discuss religion. She encouraged men and women to think critically about what the church authorities were teaching. She was put on trial, sentenced to excommunication, and banished from the colony.

When Roger Williams, a pastor in Salem, dared to question some of the Puritan teachings, he, too, was expelled from the colony. Williams went south to what is now Rhode Island, where he founded the city of Providence and started his own church.

In Puritan Massachusetts, membership in the Society of Friends, or Quakers, was a crime punishable by death. Mary Dyer, a Quaker, left the Massachusetts Bay Colony with Anne Hutchinson and lived for a while in Rhode Island. More than once, she made the mistake of returning to Boston and was arrested each time. On June 1, 1660, Mary Dyer (above) was publicly hanged on Boston Common.

In many parts of the world, religious people believed that some people were witches who conspired with the devil. These beliefs led to mob hysteria. Nowhere was the superstition and fear more violent than in Salem, Massachusetts. An epidemic of accusations in 1692 led to the execution of twenty people in Salem and dozens more in other parts of the colony.

In time, sanity prevailed and the colonial governor stopped the witch trials. The iron rule of the Puritan leaders was beginning to crumble. ■

tribes to join him in raids on the colony, and a three-year war spread through much of New England. Several hundred people on both sides were killed.

Trading on the High Seas

The Plymouth Colony was absorbed into the Massachusetts Bay Colony late in the seventeenth century. Also, Massachusetts had purchased coastal lands in what is now Maine. By 1700, there were about 30,000 colonists in Massachusetts and some 260,000 English people in America. Boston was the major city in the colonies, with a population of about 7,000.

Most colonists lived within 100 miles (161 km) of the seacoast. About 90 percent of the people were farmers; the others were fishers, sailors, clergymen, merchants, and lumbermen. In those days, everyone had to be self-sufficient—sort of jacks-of-all-trades. It was difficult and costly to find someone else to provide goods or services.

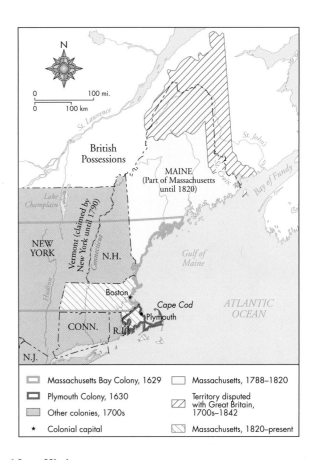

Historical map of Massachusetts

Fortunes were made by colonial shipowners whose fleets carried goods across the ocean. A so-called Triangular Trade developed. Large sugar plantations in the West Indies were tended by African slaves. Massachusetts ships sailed to the islands to pick up molasses made from the sugar. They carried the molasses to Boston, where it was used to make rum. And profits from the rum were used to buy more slaves in Africa and transport them to the West Indies.

Massachusetts Firsts

Massachusetts was a leader among the early colonies in many ways. Here are some "firsts":

The first Thanksgiving celebration

The first public park, Boston Common

The first public secondary school

The first college, Harvard

The first printing press (left)

The first post office

The first ironworks

The first public library

The first regularly issued newspaper

The first lighthouse

All this happened before the American Revolution (1775–1783). The first battles of the Revolution were fought in Lexington and Concord. ▪

Phillis Wheatley, Poet

Slavery was not common in the northern colonies, but it was not unknown. In 1761, Susannah Wheatley of Boston bought Phillis, an African girl about eight years old, and took the child into her home. Young Phillis had a brilliant mind, and she quickly learned English and later, Latin. Although she was still a slave, she was treated almost like a member of the family and was encouraged to express herself. She was known by the family name.

Phillis Wheatley's first poem was printed in the *Newport Mercury* when she was thirteen. Later, she met many famous people and traveled to London. A book of her poems was published, and she was given her freedom. Just before the American Revolution started, Phillis Wheatley composed a poem in honor of General George Washington, and he invited her to visit him in Cambridge.

Phillis Wheatley earned a place in history as the first published American poet of African ancestry. ■

In the eyes of the English, the main purpose of the colonies was to trade with the home country. The English wanted all products grown or manufactured in the colonies to come straight to their country. Also, the English Parliament wanted all goods sold in the colonies, wherever they came from, to pass through English ports and be carried on English ships. This conflict over trade was a major cause of the American Revolution.

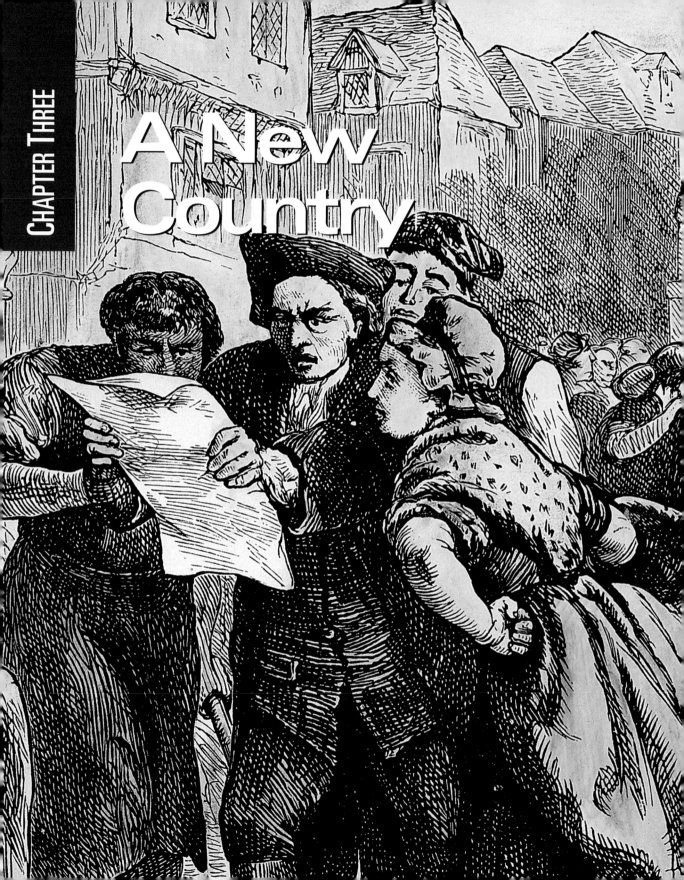

CHAPTER THREE

A New Country

Fights between colonists and British soldiers broke out because of the Stamp Act.

One hundred fifty years after the landing of the Pilgrims, nearly 250,000 people were living in the Massachusetts colony. Times had been good for some of them.

Britain was at war with other European nations during much of the eighteenth century, and by 1760, Britain controlled most of North America. None of the fighting took place in Massachusetts, however. Some colonists, such as merchants, shipowners, and lawyers actually profited from the wars.

Britain regarded the colonies as part of the British Empire and expected the people to be loyal to the king and Parliament and work for the good of Britain. But more and more colonists in North America were beginning to feel quite separate from the mother country. Some even called themselves "Americans."

The Intolerable Acts

Britain wanted to reap more profits from colonial trade, and Parliament passed several laws that the colonists resented. The Sugar Act (1764) placed a tax on molasses entering the colonies from ports outside the British Empire. The Stamp Act levied taxes on newspapers and other publications, on legal documents, and even on playing cards.

Opposite: Angry colonists read the notice of the Stamp Act.

Crispus Attucks was killed in a skirmish with British Soldiers.

Other laws threatened personal freedoms and rights the colonists had enjoyed as British citizens. Colonists began to call the repressive laws the Intolerable Acts. The people of Massachusetts strongly believed in the idea of government by the people. They didn't want all their laws to come from London.

Fights broke out from time to time between colonists and British soldiers stationed in Boston. During one of these skirmishes, on March 5, 1770, Crispus Attucks, a man of African descent, was one of several Bostonians killed. The Revolutionary leader and Founding Father Samuel Adams and his friends called this street fight the Boston Massacre.

In 1773, Parliament irritated the colonists again. A new law gave the East India Company a monopoly on the sale of tea in the American colonies. In protest, ports up and down the coast refused to let British tea be brought ashore.

Bostonians reacted differently. In an incident later called the Boston Tea Party, Samuel Adams and his friends raided British ships in Boston Harbor and dumped their cargoes of tea overboard. Parliament retaliated by closing the port of Boston.

A Continental Congress

The colonists were shocked at Parliament's reaction. Virginia's Assembly of Burgesses (colonial legislature) proposed that the colonies form a congress to decide what to do about the situation.

All the colonies except Georgia sent delegates to the Continental Congress. Fifty-six men met in Philadelphia on September 5, 1774. Four were from Massachusetts, including Samuel Adams and his cousin John Adams. The Congress made several

Opposite: Colonists, dressed as American Indians, destroyed tea in Boston Harbor.

Samuel Adams

Samuel Adams was a fanatic and a radical. He was also an important Founding Father of this country, serving as a member of the First and Second Continental Congresses and later as governor of Massachusetts.

Adams has been called the greatest plotter of revolution America has ever seen. He devoted fifteen years of his life to persuading American colonists to rise up against British rule.

Sam Adams was not very successful at business or the law, but he knew how to pull people together for a cause. While serving in the colonial legislature, he organized a protest against the Stamp Act. He formed committees and used newspapers and town meetings to promote anti-British ideas.

Adams repeated slogans over and over to make his point. "Tyranny and slavery" and "No taxation without representation" became rallying cries. ■

important decisions: to ask Parliament to repeal the Intolerable Acts, to declare the colonies would not obey them, and to prohibit all trade between the colonies and Great Britain. Committees were to be chosen in every town to see that the boycott was honored.

"The Shot Heard round the World"

Before the Congress could convene a second time, the colonies were in a shooting war with Great Britain. It started in Massachusetts, when the king's troops were ordered to seize armaments belonging to the colonies. The patriots heard of the orders, and Paul Revere and William Dawes were sent out to warn the countryside that the British were coming.

Fights broke out between British soldiers and citizens of Massachusetts at Lexington and Concord on April 19, 1775. In May when the Congress met again, George Washington, a planter from Virginia,

At the Concord Monument

In memory of the first skirmishes in the American Revolution, Ralph Waldo Emerson wrote a hymn to be sung at the completion of the Concord Monument on April 19, 1836. This is the first stanza:

*By the rude bridge that
  arched the flood,
Their flag to April's
  breeze unfurled,
Here once the embat-
  tled farmers stood,
And fired the shot heard
  round the world.* ■

was chosen to lead the Continental army, and war was declared against Great Britain.

A little more than 2 million people were living in the colonies at this time. According to John Adams, at least one-third of them were opposed to separation from Britain, but it was too late to avoid. Nearly 100,000 colonists left, mostly for Canada. These people were called Tories or Loyalists.

On June 17, 1775, the colonists and British soldiers fought the first major engagement of the American Revolution on two hills across the Charles River from Boston. The British won the Battle of Bunker Hill, but the cost was very high. More than four of every ten Redcoats (so called because of their bright red uniforms) were killed or wounded.

Shays' Rebellion

In Massachusetts, the state government was largely controlled by the merchants of Boston. Meanwhile, farmers were in deep financial trouble after the Revolution, facing foreclosures and loss of their farms. Many were veterans of the war, and in 1786, their discontent exploded.

Daniel Shays, a veteran, led some of the farmers on a march against the arsenal in Springfield. The aim was to overthrow the state government. After about a month of skirmishes, the state militia brought an end to the rebellion. Legal battles kept the courts busy for several more months. ■

Creating a Nation

The Continental Congress met again in May 1776, after the fighting had started. They adopted the Declaration of Independence in July, then began establishing a government. The Articles of Confederation were adopted in November, but they were not ratified by all the colonies for more than three years. There was no central or federal government—each colony, or state, was on its own.

The war continued for seven more years. Boston-born Benjamin Franklin persuaded the French government to help the colonies. Toward the end of the war, he met with negotiators from London to work out peace terms. He and John Jay, from New York, signed the Treaty of Paris in 1783, which finally recognized the independence of the thirteen colonies.

The Revolution was over, and the thirteen American colonies were free of British rule. Massachusetts (including the territory that is today the state of Maine) was now a self-governing commonwealth with its own constitution, adopted in 1780 by vote of the citizens in town meetings. Most of the other colonies had also adopted new constitutions.

An unfinished sketch of Benjamin Franklin (center) preparing to sign the Treaty of Paris.

But how were these thirteen governments going to work together?

George Washington and other leaders were deeply concerned about the rebellion in Massachusetts stirred up by Daniel Shays. Washington saw the need for a union of states with power that went beyond the weak Articles of Confederation.

A convention was organized and scheduled to meet in Philadelphia in May 1787. Washington was elected to chair the meeting. The delegates worked quickly, and by September, they had produced and approved a constitution. It would go into effect as soon as nine states had ratified it. Massachusetts was the sixth state to vote for ratification, on February 6, 1788. Four months later, New Hampshire was the ninth.

The Freedom Trail

The Freedom Trail, a walking tour through downtown Boston, is marked in red on the sidewalks. Major landmarks that commemorate the role of this city during the Colonial and Revolutionary periods are included.

The Granary Burying Ground has the graves of John Hancock, Paul Revere, Samuel Adams, and other leaders. The site of the first free public school is also marked. Across the street from this site stands a statue of Benjamin Franklin.

The Old Globe Corner Bookstore, built in 1712, is one of the oldest buildings in the city. Many town meetings were held at Old South Meeting House to discuss the situation with the British. Some of these meetings led to the planning of the Boston Tea Party.

The Old State House, built in 1729, was the meeting place of the royal governor and colonial legislature. The Boston Massacre took place just outside this building. The Declaration of Independence was first read to the citizens of Boston from its balcony in 1776, a ceremony that is repeated every Fourth of July.

Faneuil Hall Marketplace is called the Cradle of Liberty because it was used for mass meetings prior to the American Revolution. Today, people enjoy shops, restaurants, food stalls, and vending carts in this historic spot.

The seventeenth-century home of Paul Revere has been preserved, and nearby is Old North Church. The patriots had arranged a signal to let Paul Revere and William Dawes know when the British were about to seize the arms stored by the colonists. A lantern hung in the tower of Old North Church was the signal. The time had come. The two men took off on horseback to Lexington and Concord, and the colonists were ready for a fight when the British arrived the next day.

Two Freedom Trail landmarks are across the Charles River, in Charlestown. A tall monument commerates the Battle of Bunker Hill, and "Old Ironsides," the USS *Constitution,* is in Charlestown Navy Yard. ■

World Trade

Once the Treaty of Paris was signed, American merchants—no longer restricted by Parliament—were ready to trade with the world. In November 1783, a new merchant ship sailed out of New York Harbor, bound for China.

Within the next few years, ships were sailing regularly from Boston, Newburyport, and Salem to countries in Africa and Asia. They brought back jade, silks, tea, and spices for sale in America. They took codfish, whale oil, lumber, and produce to the West Indies to trade for cocoa, sugar, tobacco, and molasses. South America and the Pacific Northwest provided even more markets.

World events interrupted the progress of this prosperous shipping industry. The young United States found itself at war with Britain again in the War of 1812 (1812–1815). The USS *Constitution*, America's first warship, took part in three major sea battles with the Royal Navy. That ship, nicknamed "Old Ironsides," is now entirely restored and on display in Charlestown Harbor, near Bunker Hill.

The USS *Constitution,* "Old Ironsides"

The Industrial Revolution

The war seriously slowed down the state's busy international trade. Massachusetts businessmen began to realize they should look for other sources of wealth besides shipping.

In 1810, a prosperous merchant named Francis Cabot Lowell took a trip to Manchester, England. Manchester was a busy industrial city, where many mills turned out huge quantities of textiles for markets in many countries.

Lowell, who had a phenomenal memory, carefully observed how the machinery worked. When he got home, he formed a com-

The Adams Family

Few families had as much influence on early American history as the Adams family of Massachusetts. Samuel and his cousin John were fourth-generation residents of Massachusetts, and both men were strong advocates of independence from England. John Adams (left) was more thoughtful and less feisty than Samuel, but he was just as determined. He was the leader in getting the Continental Congress to accept the Declaration of Independence, written by Thomas Jefferson.

John Adams became the new nation's first vice president. Often called the "Crown Prince," he then succeeded George Washington as president. John's wife, Abigail (right), was a strong and influential woman. She was an advocate for women's rights and spoke out against slavery long before these topics became national issues. "Remember the ladies," she wrote in a letter to her husband. "Be more generous and favorable to them than your ancestors. Do not put such unlimited power in the hands of the husbands."

John and Abigail's son, John Quincy Adams, became the sixth president of the United States, and his son, Charles Francis Adams, was President Abraham Lincoln's ambassador to Great Britain. Two of Charles's sons, Brooks Adams and Henry Truslow Adams, enjoyed distinguished careers as scholars and writers.

The Adams National Historic Site in Quincy includes three historic Adams family homes.

pany and hired a mechanic. He described what he wanted, and the mechanic was able to construct it. In 1814, Lowell was ready to operate the first power loom in America and one of the first factories.

The textile industry grew so fast that the investors soon needed to build more mills. East Chelmsford (later renamed Lowell), where the Merrimack and Concord Rivers meet, had what was needed—water for power and for navigation.

Lowell died in 1817, but he had set in motion the beginning of the Industrial Revolution in Massachusetts. The nineteenth century saw the rapid development of manufacturing in the state. Many farmers left their lands for better opportunities in the factories.

Shipping, shipbuilding, whaling, and manufacturing made Massachusetts a thriving state by the middle of the nineteenth century. Donald McKay of Boston was the foremost builder of a new, fast type of merchant ship called the clipper.

The Barre Slave Case

In 1783, Quork Walker, a black slave from the little town of Barre, sued his master for assault and battery. The Supreme Court of Massachusetts decided the master had no right to beat Walker. They declared him a free man and awarded him fifty pounds in damages. Slavery was not legal in Massachusetts from then on, and by 1790, there were no slaves in the state. ■

Textile mills were the economic mainstay of Lowell in the 1800s.

Journalist William
Lloyd Garrison

Reform Movements

Abolitionists were one of several reform groups who spoke out against slavery during the nineteenth century. William Lloyd Garrison, a Boston journalist, published a paper called *The Liberator*. From its first issue in 1831 until the Civil War, *The Liberator* was a leading voice against slavery.

Slavery had almost entirely disappeared in the northern states by 1800, so many runaway slaves made their way to Massachusetts. It was easy for them to find people there who would help them escape the bounty hunters who searched for them.

Garrison was also an advocate of women's suffrage. Worcester, in central Massachusetts, became a center of feminist activity and agitation. In 1850, the first national Women's Rights Convention attracted some 1,100 delegates from eleven states. The theme was liberation—for women as well as for slaves.

Along with antislavery and women's rights, reform leaders worked to improve education and conditions in prisons, public hospitals, and institutions for the mentally ill and physically handicapped.

The Civil War

More than 150,000 men from Massachusetts served in the Union army and navy during the Civil War (1861–1865). Many Union ships were built and equipped in the state's shipyards.

The 54th Massachusetts Volunteer Infantry was the nation's first African-American regiment. Led by Colonel Robert Gould Shaw, a Boston abolitionist, the outfit took part in several battles. Sergeant William Carney of the 54th became the first African-American to receive the Congressional Medal of Honor.

More Massachusetts Firsts

Massachusetts continued to achieve many "firsts" during the nineteenth century. The state was changing from an agricultural to an industrial society.

1832: The first school in the nation for blind children opened in Boston.

1837: The first state hospital for the mentally ill was established in Worcester. Mount Holyoke College, the first women's college in the nation, was founded.

1839: Rubber was first vulcanized by Charles Goodyear in Woburn.

1846: The first lockstitch sewing machine was made in Boston, by Elias Howe.

1875: The first American Christmas card was printed in Boston.

1876: The first telephone in America was demonstrated by Alexander Graham Bell (right) in Boston.

1886: The world's first electric power transformer was demonstrated in Boston by William Stanley.

1893: The first successful gasoline-powered automobile was perfected by Charles and Frank Duryea, in Springfield.

1897: The first American subway system was opened in Boston. ■

"Banned in Boston"

A new kind of Puritanism sprang up in Boston in 1878, when the New England Society for the Suppression of Vice was established. The goal of the group, later renamed the Watch and Ward Society, was the "suppression of all agencies tending to corrupt the morals of youth."

After some success in the fight against crime and corruption, the society turned its attention to obscenity, "immodest advertising," and immoral literature. Their fight to ban the sale of many books and plays became a form of censorship that threatened the basic principle of freedom of speech. The phrase "banned in Boston" came to stand for anything that was the least bit controversial.

The Puritan forefathers would have approved.

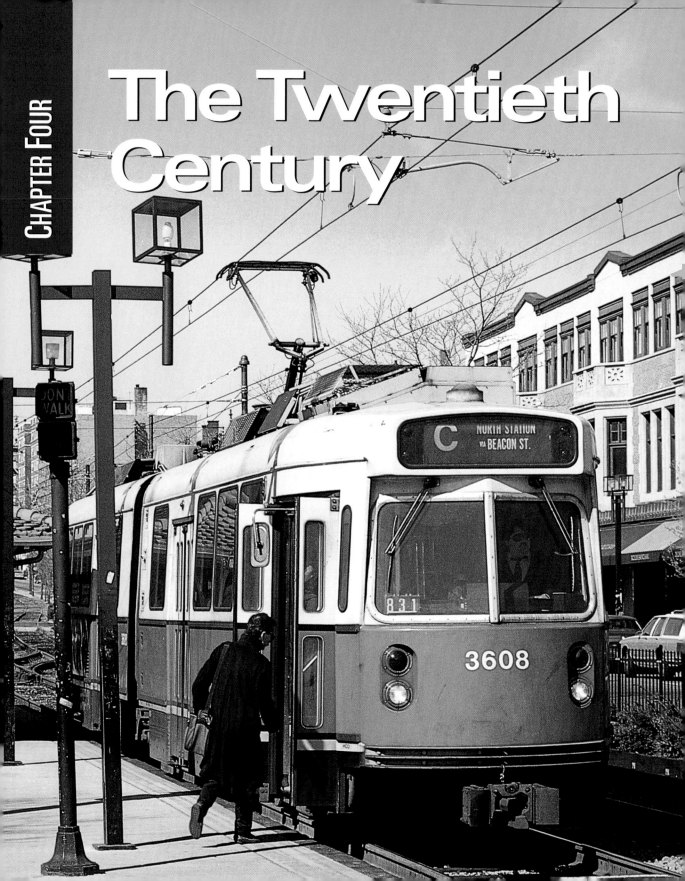

CHAPTER FOUR

The Twentieth Century

The Stanley Steamer

About 2.5 million people lived in Massachusetts around 1900. Nearly one-third of them had come to this country as immigrants in search of a better life.

The horse-drawn carriage was on its way out. Inventors had been experimenting with motorized carriages for several decades, and now, automobiles were about to change the face of the nation. The most successful Massachusetts automobile manufacturers were twin brothers Francis and Freelan Stanley. They manufactured the Stanley Steamer (a steam-powered automobile) from 1897 to 1924.

Electric trolley lines provided public transportation in the city of Boston. They were so popular that they created traffic jams in the center of the city. This problem was partly solved by the opening of the nation's first subway, which ran underneath Boston Common.

Opposite: Electric light-rail systems provide public transportation around Boston.

Textile mills were dangerous workplaces for young and old alike.

Labor and Industry

Textile manufacturing was still a major part of Massachusetts industry, but working conditions in the mills were harsh—even dangerous. The air in the crowded factories was lint-filled, not fit to breathe. Machinery was deafeningly noisy. And wages were so low that families could barely afford to eat, even when both parents and one or more children worked in the mills.

In 1912, workers in Lawrence found their pay had been cut because new laws had shortened the workweek. They went on strike for two months and won a small pay raise and other concessions. One striker carried a banner that read, "We want bread, but we want roses, too." The incident is remembered as the "Bread and Roses" strike.

The end of World War I (1914–1918) resulted in falling wages and rising prices. Workers were not happy. There were some 3,600 strikes in the United States that year, in all kinds of industries.

In Boston, police officers joined the American Federation of Labor in the hope of improving their wages and working conditions. When the police commissioner fired some of the organizers, their fellow police officers walked off their jobs. Left with no police protection, the city experienced violence and looting. Governor Calvin Coolidge called out the National Guard to put down the strike.

Between Two Wars

Massachusetts had profited from manufacturing for more than 100 years, but times were changing. Textile and shoe manufacturers were moving to southern states, where workers would accept lower wages.

Frances Perkins

Boston-born Frances Perkins became the first woman member of the U.S. Cabinet when President Franklin D. Roosevelt appointed her secretary of labor in 1933. Perkins had graduated from Mount Holyoke College and had become a teacher, then a social worker.

Her public career started in New York State, where she served on the state industrial commission. She worked to improve conditions for factory workers, especially women and children.

During her twelve-year service as secretary of labor, Perkins helped promote such programs as social security, federal relief, minimum wage, maximum hours, and the abolition of child labor. ■

The Great Depression would have been even more disastrous without the public works programs that gave some relief to unemployed workers. The state of Massachusetts initiated unemployment programs in 1929. The federal government, under President Franklin D. Roosevelt, started several programs that gave additional help.

World War II (1939–1945) brought boom times to southern New England. Factories and shipyards were kept busy round the clock, producing huge amounts of supplies and armaments for the war.

The General Electric plant in Lynn began production of the first U.S. jet engine in 1942. Meanwhile, scientists from Harvard and the Massachusetts Institute of Technology (MIT) were teaming up with industry and defense personnel to design and build the first computers.

An MIT laboratory research computer in the late 1940s

The Fifties

Just as automobiles had changed the face of America fifty years earlier, computers and television led the country into the electronic age. New England's first TV station, WBZ-TV, went on the air in Boston in 1948.

Important breakthroughs in medicine were made by Massachusetts scientists. Dr. Joseph E. Murray of Milford performed the first successful human kidney transplant in 1953. He shared the 1990 Nobel Prize for physiology or medicine for his work.

In 1957, the Worcester Foundation, founded by Clark University professors Dr. Hudson Hoagland and Dr. Gregory G. Pincus, announced the successful testing of "the Pill." This birth-control method is widely used throughout the world today.

The 1950s saw great architectural changes in the city of Boston. An urban-renewal program transformed a neighborhood of narrow streets, saloons, burlesque halls, and old tenements into a center of modern office buildings and luxury apartments. Fortunately, a few of Boston's historic buildings in the region were preserved.

Dr. Hudson Hoagland

Another Massachusetts President

The Kennedys were probably the best-known American family in the world during the last half of the 1900s. Joseph P. Kennedy and Rose Fitzgerald Kennedy, who lived in Brookline, had nine children. Joseph was a highly successful businessman, and Rose came from a political family. Her father, John F. Fitzgerald, was twice mayor of Boston, the first son of Irish parents to hold that office.

There was intense rivalry in Boston between the Protestant elite, many of them descended from early colonists, and the rapidly

Dr. Gregory G. Pincus

The Kennedy clan at Hyannis Port in 1948 (John F., far left; Joe, center; Robert F., second from right; and Teddy, front)

increasing Irish Catholic population. Most of the old-timers, nicknamed the Boston Brahmins, were Republicans. The Irish Catholics were solidly behind the Democratic Party.

The Kennedy family brought Massachusetts into the forefront of American politics. Like the Adams family several generations earlier, their influence on the state and the nation spanned many years.

Joe and Rose Kennedy had high ambitions for their sons. The story of the Kennedy family is one of great achievements, but it is also full of incredible tragedy. Their oldest son, Joseph, was killed in England while serving in World War II. Kathleen, the second daughter, died a short time later in an airplane crash.

John Fitzgerald Kennedy (JFK), the second son, was a war hero. He started his political career in 1946, when he was elected to the U.S. House of Representatives. He served three terms, then challenged the Republican incumbent, Henry Cabot Lodge, for his seat in the Senate. To the surprise of many people, Kennedy won and was reelected to the Senate in 1958.

By 1960, JFK was ready to run for the presidency. At that time, prejudice against both Irish and Catholics was strong in many parts of the country, but Kennedy's campaign was highly organized, efficient, and well financed. He won the Democratic nomination and went on to defeat Richard M. Nixon for the presidency.

The whole nation was in deep shock three years later when President Kennedy was assassinated in Dallas, Texas, on November 22, 1963.

Civil Rights

The 1960s were turbulent years for the United States. The civil rights struggle was front-page news week after week. Robert Kennedy, John's younger brother, while serving as attorney general of the United States, helped enforce federal laws to uphold the

John F. Kennedy with women voters during his first campaign for the House of Representatives

Edward Brooke

In 1966, Massachusetts elected Edward William Brooke to the U.S. Senate. Winning by 500,000 votes, he became the first black U.S. senator since Reconstruction, the years following the Civil War. His election was especially impressive because he was a Protestant and a Republican in a predominantly Catholic and Democratic state. Reelected in 1972, he represented the state for twelve years.

A graduate of Howard University and Boston University Law School, Brooke served as attorney general of the state from 1963 until he went to the Senate. He was known as a strong fighter against corruption and organized crime.

Senator Brooke worked for antipoverty legislation and a strengthening of the Social Security system. He received honorary degrees from several colleges and awards for his leadership from the Junior Chamber of Commerce, the National Association for the Advancement of Colored People (NAACP), and the National Conference of Christians and Jews. ■

Robert Kennedy answering questions from the press

rights of African-Americans to vote and to attend previously all white schools.

The youngest Kennedy brother, Edward (Ted), was elected to John's Senate seat in 1962. In spite of a scandal that involved a drowning in 1969, Massachusetts voters reelected "Teddy" time and time again. He consistently supported civil rights, social programs for the poor, and other liberal legislation.

Robert Kennedy was elected to the U.S. Senate from New York in 1964, where he worked to help minorities and was critical of the Vietnam War. He decided to run for the presidency in 1968, but during the campaign, he was shot and killed by an assassin.

Few Boston schools were racially integrated in the 1960s, even after many civil rights victories in other parts of the country. In 1972, a group of African-American parents and the NAACP took the matter to the federal district court. In 1974, a judge declared that Boston schools were "unconstitutionally segregated."

Following this decision, attempts were made to integrate the schools by busing children from one section of the city to another. Many white working-class parents were opposed to forced busing. The rift between Boston's African-Americans and the South Boston Irish created by this action was slow to heal.

Angry parents protest forced busing in Boston.

1972 Election

The presidential election of 1972 was the biggest landslide of the century. Incumbent Republican president Richard M. Nixon won the popular vote by nearly two to one against his challenger, Senator George McGovern.

Only Massachusetts and the District of Columbia voted for the Democratic candidate. Republicans had a good time poking fun at the Democrats of Massachusetts. But when scandals forced President Nixon to resign from office, the tables were turned. Bumper stickers appeared on Bay State cars that read, "Don't Blame Me, I'm from Massachusetts." ■

Cheers

Beginning in 1983, Boston came into the homes of television viewers everywhere through a series named *Cheers,* about a fictional saloon of the same name. Its 275 episodes were aired over 11 seasons.

The rest of the country got to hear Boston accents and meet some of its fictional residents. Several *Cheers* stars went on to other successes in TV and film.

Boston politicians loved *Cheers.* Massachusetts governor William Weld honored the television program by proclaiming an official Cheers Day when it went off the air. ◼

Recent Elections

Michael S. Dukakis, a native of Brookline whose parents were immigrants from Greece, had a long and successful political career in Massachusetts. He served four terms in the state legislature, starting in 1962, and three terms as governor of the state. The state's economy improved during his time in office but took a downturn later. Dukakis was the Democratic candidate for the U.S. presidency in 1988, but he lost to Republican George Bush, who was also born in Massachusetts.

In 1993, Boston elected Thomas Merino, of Italian descent, its first non–Irish-American mayor since 1929. Two popular Massachusetts political figures ran for the U.S. Senate in 1996. Republican governor William Weld tried, unsuccessfully, to unseat the Democratic incumbent, John F. Kerry.

Michael S. Dukakis delivers his State of the State address to a joint session of the legislature.

Shores, Valleys, and Hills

Massachusetts is a slice of New England that reaches from the Atlantic Ocean to New York State. Its western boundary and much of its northern and southern boundaries are straight lines. In the northeast, the state border curves north for a few miles, and in the east and southeast, the ocean creates a jagged coastline. Vermont and New Hampshire make up the northern boundary of the state. New York is on the west, and Connecticut and Rhode Island make up most of the southern border.

The coastline, with its hundreds of inlets and bays along the Atlantic Ocean, gives Massachusetts its longest border—and its nickname, the Bay State. Nantucket and Martha's Vineyard are the state's largest islands. Several smaller ones are called the Elizabeth Islands. Other small islands lie along the Atlantic coast.

The state's most unusual geographic feature is Cape Cod—a long, hook-shaped peninsula that curves northward from Buz-

Opposite: Water lilies, Cape Cod National Seashore

Cape Cod National Seashore

Henry David Thoreau called Cape Cod the "bare and bended arm of Massachusetts." Today, that arm is one of the most popular weekend and vacation destinations in the northeastern United States. Because the curved peninsula is so long and narrow and because most people arrive by car, traffic congestion during summer months is remarkably heavy.

Glacial action created a marvelous variety of landscape and seascape on Cape Cod, ranging from sandy beaches, dunes, and tidal flats to cliffs, marshes, ponds, and woodlands. In 1961, Congress took action to preserve a part of the cape's beauty. A 40-mile (64-km) ribbon of land along the 70-mile (112-km) peninsula was set aside as a national seashore—closed to any further development. Today, this area has hiking and biking trails, long sandy beaches, and picnic areas. Beach plums, cranberry bushes, salt spray roses, and grasses grow undisturbed among the pines, beeches, cedars, and red maples, while pond lilies and cattails thrive in the wetlands.

Cape Cod National Seashore (above) is a regular stopover along the Atlantic flyway for millions of shorebirds, gulls (below), terns, ducks, geese, and swans. Some spend the winter here, and more than 300 species of birds have been recorded. ■

zards Bay to Provincetown. While most of the state's coastline faces east along the ocean, the shores of Cape Cod and the islands face all directions—north, east, south, and west.

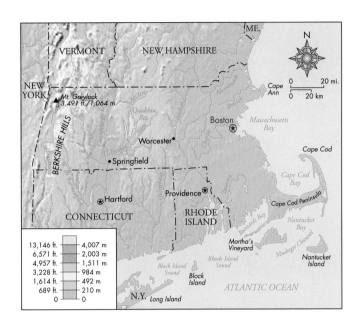

Massachusetts's topography

The Coastal Lowlands

Massachusetts has four major landforms—the Coastal Lowlands, the New England Upland, the Connecticut River Valley, and the Berkshires. These are all part of larger regions of New England.

The Coastal Lowlands cover more than one-third of the state, extending inland from the ocean. This is a region of low hills and many swamps, lakes, ponds, and rivers. Patches of fertile soil are found in the lower areas.

Most of the state's rivers are short and shallow, but the mighty Merrimack in the north has played an important part in the region's history. Other major rivers in the Coastal Lowlands are the Charles, Nashua, Concord, and Taunton. Much of the soil is too rocky for good farming. One crop, however, does very well in this region—cranberries. Much of the shoreline is rocky, but Massachusetts has several fine, well-sheltered harbors.

The land on Cape Cod and the islands is called a coastal plain. Part of the cape is a ridge formed by glacial deposits, called a *moraine.*

Walden Pond, an Environmental Symbol

A small pond covering less than 1/2 square mile (1.3 sq km) is one of the best-known natural landmarks in Massachusetts. Walden Pond (above), now part of a state reservation, has been a popular recreation spot for more than 100 years.

Henry David Thoreau (above, inset), a writer and philosopher who lived in Concord, spent a couple of years in a tiny wooden cabin on the pond. He swam and hiked, read and wrote, played the flute, and raised a garden. His book, *Walden,* was published in 1854. In it he wrote about living close to nature. He believed that his experiences living close to nature helped him understand himself and society.

Thoreau's thoughts about wilderness preservation and peaceful resistance to evils in society have influenced many world leaders. Civil rights leader Martin Luther King Jr., India's Mahatma Gandhi, and environmentalist John Muir, who helped promote forest conservation in the United States, were all influenced by Thoreau's writings about life on Walden Pond.

Today, the pond is almost "loved to death." Each weekend, thousands of people crowd into the parking lot at the reservation. The state of Massachusetts does its best, with limited funds, to preserve this historic and inspirational spot. ■

The New England Upland

West of the Coastal Lowlands is the New England Upland, a hilly region that stretches from Maine to New Jersey. It is split in two sections in Massachusetts. East of the Connecticut River, the land is considered an extension of New Hampshire's White Mountains region, although the hills are not nearly as high or rocky.

Mountains made of rock that stand alone and are not part of a range of mountains are known as *monadnocks*. There are several such solitary mountains in the Eastern New England Upland.

Connecticut River Valley

The uplands are divided by the Connecticut River. It forms much of the boundary between New Hampshire and Vermont, then proceeds south through Massachusetts and Connecticut to Long Island Sound. The valley created by this river varies in width from 3 to 20 miles (5 to 32 km). The land, which rises in levels, like terraces, on each side of the valley, is the best farmland in Massachusetts, with rich soil and a milder climate than much of New England.

The Connecticut River winds through the Turner Falls area of Massachusetts.

A view from the
summit of Mt. Everett

The Berkshires

The region between the Connecticut River and the western edge of Massachusetts is most often referred to as the Berkshires. Geographically, the region consists of three separate landforms: the Western Uplands, the Berkshire Valley, and the Taconic Range. The Western Uplands have the highest mountains in Massachusetts. Mount Greylock at 3,491

Geographical Features of Massachusetts

Total area; rank	9,241 sq. mi. (23,934 sq km); 45th
Land; rank	7,838 sq. mi. (20,300 sq km); 45th
Water; rank	1,403 sq. mi. (3,634 sq km); 21st
Inland water; **rank**	424 sq. mi. (1,098 sq km); 35th
Coastal water; **rank**	979 sq. mi. (2,536 sq km); 7th
Geographic center	Worcester
Highest point	Mount Greylock, 3,491 feet (1,064 m)
Lowest point	Sea level along Atlantic coast
Largest city	Boston
Longest river	Connecticut River, 66 miles (106 km)
Population; rank	6,029,051 (1990 census); 13th
Record high temperature	107°F (42°C) at New Bedford and Chester on August 2, 1975
Record low temperature	−34°F (−37°C) at Birch Hill Dam on January 18, 1957
Average July temperature	71°F (22°C)
Average January temperature	25°F (−4°C)
Average annual precipitation	45 inches (114 cm)

Webster and Webster Lake

Most place-names in Massachusetts came from places in England or from Native American names. One of the few exceptions is the town of Webster.

Daniel Webster (right), a prominent lawyer, politician, and orator, was born in New Hampshire and elected by that state to three terms in the U.S. Congress. In 1816, he moved to Boston, where he became famous as an outstanding lawyer and orator. He was elected to the U.S. House of Representatives from Massachusetts in 1823 and to the Senate four years later. Senator Webster supported the economic interests of Massachusetts manufacturers. He later ran unsuccessfully for the presidency and served two presidents as secretary of state.

The town of Webster was originally a part of Oxford, named after Oxford, England. However, Samuel Slater, a Rhode Island cotton manufacturer, established a factory there and then founded a town—and named it for Daniel Webster.

A lake in the town has two names. It is often simply called Webster Lake, but its official name, given to it by the Nipmuc people, is Chargoggagog-gmanchuaggagoggchaubuna-gungamaug, which means, "You fish your side of the lake. I fish my side. Nobody fishes the middle."

As the longest place-name in

Massachusetts, it poses a problem for mapmakers. That's why the unofficial name, Webster Lake, appears on some maps. ■

feet (1,064 m) tops the list. These mountains are an extension of Vermont's Green Mountains.

Both the Berkshire Valley and the Taconic Range are narrow strips, running from north to south. Dairy cows graze in the fertile green meadows of the Berkshire Valley. The Housatonic River runs through most of this valley and continues south through Connecticut.

The Taconic Range, a strip less than 6 miles (10 km) across, is part of a chain of mountains running north on the New York side of the border into southwestern Vermont. These mountains are a little lower than those on the other side of the Berkshire Valley.

Plant and Animal Life

About 70 percent of the land in Massachusetts is covered with forests. Early settlers cut down many trees for farmland and fuel and to build houses and ships. When better farmland was found farther west, the trees began to grow back. The most common hardwoods are ash, beech, birch, maple, and oak trees. Hardwood, or deciduous, trees have leaves. Coniferous, or evergreen, trees in Massachusetts are mostly pines and hemlocks.

Sugar maples and ash during the fall near Williamstown

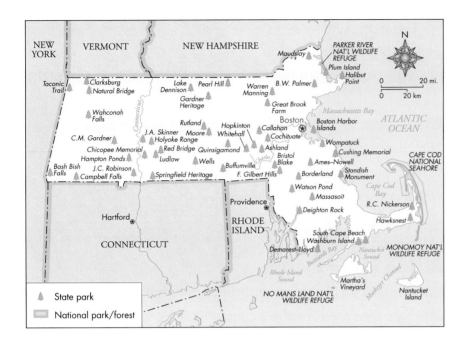

Massachusetts parks and forests

Flowering trees and bushes such as dogwoods, mountain laurels, and azaleas bring splashes of color to the woods and forests in spring. Native wildflowers include trailing arbutus, trilliums, and violets. Many kinds of ferns, rushes, and marsh grasses are found in low-lying areas.

The Cobble, a national natural landmark on the Housatonic River, has nearly 500 types of wildflowers. It also has 100 kinds of trees, shrubs, and vines; and 40 species of ferns.

Except for deer, large mammals are rare in Massachusetts today. However, black bears, bobcats, and coyotes have been spotted occasionally in the Berkshires. Smaller creatures include rabbits, squirrels, foxes, beavers, porcupines, woodchucks, mice, bats, and snakes. The forests and wetlands attract hundreds of species of birds.

The early settlers found an abundance of fish in the ocean waters off Cape Cod. Unfortunately, overfishing has greatly diminished the supply of the popular cod in recent years.

Climate

The climate in Massachusetts varies from region to region. In the western part of the state, winters are cold, averaging 21°F (−6°C) with moderately heavy snowfalls. Around Boston and the coastline, the weather is milder. There, summer temperatures average 72°F (22°C) and winter temperatures 29°F (−2°C). The weather along the coast can become quite dramatic. Storms coming from the south called northeasters can bring heavy rain and snow. Hurricanes are also occasionally a concern, with especially destructive storms battering the state in 1938, 1944, and 1985.

The blizzard of 1978 covered the entire state with 2 to 4 feet (68 to 121 cm) of snow.

Natural Disasters

Massachusetts residents have many tales to tell of two memorable storms: the Great Hurricane of 1938 and the Blizzard of 1978.

The greatest Massachusetts storm on record roared up the Atlantic coast in 1938. It seemed to come without warning—weather stations then did not have the tracking and communications systems used today. The Great Hurricane killed about 600 people on Long Island and in New England. Most of the victims were swept into the ocean by the violent winds.

Homes were destroyed, automobiles blown over, and trees toppled. The trees lost in New England would have furnished enough lumber to build 200,000 homes.

Almost forty years later, another kind of storm hit. A blizzard covered the state with a snowfall that ranged from 27 to 48 inches (68 to 121 cm). Property losses were close to $1 billion, and 29 people died.

Many commuters were trapped in their cars overnight. One estimate said that as many as 3,000 automobiles were stranded. ■

CHAPTER SIX

Here and There around the State

Nine out of ten Bay Staters live in the large megalopolis that includes most of northeastern Massachusetts. A megalopolis is a densely populated region where many cities are so close to one another that they seem like one big city. Boston is the hub, or core, of that megalopolis. In fact, it has been called the Hub for a long time. Bostonians sometimes call it the Hub of the Universe.

Boston is a small city. Getting around by foot or on public transportation is very easy—if you don't get lost. Tradition says that Boston streets retrace the cowpaths of the original village. The population of the city is a little over 500,000, making it twenty-first in population among U.S. cities. An additional 5 million people live in surrounding cities.

Besides having a concentration of industrial, financial, and educational institutions, Boston has twenty-five facilities for medical research, more than any other U.S. city.

Among many outstanding points of interest are the state house, the Freedom Trail, Museum of Fine Arts, Boston Public Library, John F. Kennedy Library, and Fenway Park.

But there is much more to Massachusetts than Boston. Each city and town, including those within the megalopolis, has its own identity and its own heritage and traditions. Most of them were settled soon after Plymouth Colony was founded. Historical museums in

The dense streets of the financial district of Boston seen from the air

Opposite: Fishing boats in the bay at Rockport

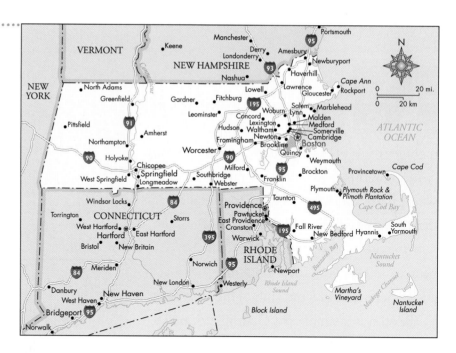

Massachusetts cities and interstates

nearly every city, town, and village are filled with artifacts that illustrate local history.

A typical Massachusetts town is neat and clean, with a pretty square, or common, in the center. Often, there is a bandstand on the common, used for outdoor concerts in summer. Colonial and early American buildings have been well preserved, and most of them are in daily use as homes, public buildings, and offices. New houses often copy traditional architecture and are built of red brick with white trim or white clapboard with dark shutters.

North of Boston

In Massachusetts, the seacoast was settled first. Newcomers sailed along the coastline in search of good harbors and large quantities of fish. The local museums or coastal towns display ship models, goods brought from ports around the world, and artifacts of the American Revolution.

A shoreline drive passes through dozens of quaint fishing villages and early towns. Views of rocky shores and ocean waves change constantly with the weather, and whales are often sighted close to land.

Cape Ann is a picturesque point of land about halfway between the New Hampshire border and the city of Boston. Rockport and Gloucester share a history as fishing villages; today, they are notable summer resorts and artists' colonies.

Salem, farther down the coast, has a notorious past because of its trials and executions of women accused of witchcraft. The 355-year-old home of a judge who presided over some of the trials is open to the public. Salem's history is much more than witch trials, however. Half a dozen buildings in Salem Maritime National Historic Site tell of Salem's days as a prosperous port and shipbuilding center.

Marblehead sits on a little finger of land next to Salem. Its beautiful harbor is full of sailboats in summer. The annual Race Week attracts yachts from many other ports.

Gloucester is a summer resort popular among both artists and fishers.

Merrimack Valley

The Greater Merrimack Valley is full of landmarks. Three important historic periods are represented—the American Revolution, the Industrial Revolution, and the years when many leading writers and thinkers lived in Concord and nearby towns.

Lawrence and Lowell were the first two industrial cities in the state. The Museum of Textile History in Lawrence and Lowell National Historical Park, tell the story of the early days of the textile industry and its workers.

The American Revolution began in Lexington and Concord on April 19, 1775. A minuteman statue stands near Concord's North Bridge, where the "shot heard round the world" was fired. Important sites are preserved in Minute Man National Historical Park. Concord is also remembered as the home of many of the nation's most important nineteenth-century writers.

The harvesting of cranberries

South of Boston

Plymouth County, between Boston and Cape Cod, was the birthplace of Massachusetts. Today, people visit the area to retrace the footsteps of the Pilgrims and to watch the harvest of millions of bright-red cranberries.

The two major cities of Bristol County are New Bedford and Fall River. New Bedford is famous as a onetime whaling center. Both cities thrived on cotton manufacturing for many decades.

Cape Cod and the Islands

In summer, thousands of visitors come to Cape Cod from Boston, New York City, Canada, and all across America. Everywhere on the cape, tourists find museums, restaurants, and attractive accommodations. Some are elegant and exclusive; some are more modest. The ocean is the main attraction in the area, of course, and every imaginable water sport is available. A fine museum in Sandwich, the oldest town on the cape, has a large collection of the pressed glass manufactured there during the nineteenth century.

Cycling is a popular summer activity on Martha's Vineyard.

Whale-watching cruises leave from Barnstable, on the North Shore, and from Provincetown. Provincetown is a lively town, with many sidewalk artists, souvenir stands, food stalls, restaurants, and motels.

Martha's Vineyard is a triangle-shaped island about 20 miles (32 km) from west to east and 10 miles (16 km) from north to south. Charming villages, sandy beaches, boat harbors, and five picturesque lighthouses make it a mecca for summer vacationers.

Ferries dock at Vineyard Haven. Oak Bluffs, once called Wesleyan Grove, started out in 1835 as a campground for Methodist church groups who held their annual gospel meetings in this beautiful place. Elegant Edgartown, with its stately mansions built by whaling captains, is now a major yachting center. It is the oldest town on the island.

The Wampanoag People

About 300 Wampanoag people live on Martha's Vineyard, half of them in the village of Gay Head. Their ancestors have lived in eastern Massachusetts for at least 600 years. During the whaling era, these Native Americans of Martha's Vineyard were in much demand as boat steerers. They had a reputation for unusual skill and courage.

Today, the people are governed by the Wampanoag Tribal Council of Gay Head, Inc. It was recognized as a legal government by United States in 1987. An additional 500 Wampanoags living in other towns in the United States and Canada are listed on the tribal rolls. The tribal council has built a center for offices and meetings, and planned projects include housing units, a museum and archive, an arts center, and an amphitheater.

The most important holiday in the year for the Gay Head Wampanoags is Cranberry Day, the second Tuesday in October. It is celebrated with daytime events, a potluck supper, and a pageant. ■

Great Point Lighthouse, Nantucket

Nantucket Island is smaller than Martha's Vineyard and farther from the Massachusetts mainland. *Nantucket* is a Native American word meaning "faraway island." At one time, eighty-eight whaling ships sailed around the world from Nantucket waters. Herman Melville's novel *Moby-Dick* (1851) was based on the true story of a Nantucket whaling ship.

Nantucket's beaches stretch for 82 miles (132 km). There are dunes, moors, three lighthouses, and a large cranberry bog on the island.

Worcester County

During the Civil War, dozens of factories along nearly every river and stream in Worcester County were turning out machinery, tools, blankets, carriages, caissons, guns, gunpowder, and camp chairs, in addition to textiles and shoes, to equip and clothe the Union army.

Worcester is New England's second-largest city. Worcester Car diners were manufactured here until 1961 and shipped to many markets. These forerunners of today's fast-food outlets had marble counters and oak woodwork. Worcester's manufactured products range from nuts to wire to farm equipment, from roller skates to shredded wheat.

Worcester has more than half a dozen first-class museums and twelve colleges. Mechanics Hall, a performance building opened in 1857, is one of the most acoustically perfect performance halls in the United States. Many famous people have performed or spoken from its stage, including authors Charles Dickens, Mark Twain, and Henry David Thoreau, as well as musicians Enrico Caruso, Antonín Dvořák, and Yo-Yo Ma.

Inside a Worcester Car diner

Two important early inventors came from Worcester County. Eli Whitney, a native of Westborough, transformed the cotton industry with his invention of the cotton gin 200 years ago. Elias Howe, of Spencer, created the first lockstitch sewing machine.

Harvard, in the northern part of the county, is in a beautiful setting. Many acres of protected land provide a habitat for great blue

Apple picking draws many tourists in the fall.

herons and Blandings turtles. Apple orchards welcome "pick your own" visitors in the fall. An added bonus is spectacular views of New Hampshire mountains dressed in splendid fall colors.

Bronson Alcott and some fellow transcendentalists (a group of free thinkers who questioned conservative religious beliefs and worked for social reform) tried to establish a utopian community in Harvard. This community attempted to put into practice their intellectual beliefs. The farmhouse they lived in is now part of the

Old Sturbridge Village

Across the state from Plimoth Plantation, the town of Sturbridge offers "time travel" into the early nineteenth century. Old Sturbridge Village is a settlement created by gathering together and restoring original buildings from towns throughout New England. Interpreters dressed in historic garb demonstrate the occupations, skills, and lifestyles of the people who lived in the region nearly 200 years ago. The homes, as well as the mill, meetinghouse, district school, bank, country store, and other places of business, are all open to the public.

Everything in Old Sturbridge Village has been carefully researched. A visit brings the past to life in an authentic and interesting manner. ■

Robert Goddard

A sixteen-year-old Worcester boy named Robert Goddard was fond of reading science-fiction novels. One of his favorites was *The War of the Worlds* (1898), by H. G. Wells, a story involving travel into outer space.

One day, when Robert was climbing a tree, he was struck with the idea that it might be possible to invent something that could actually be sent out into space. From that day on, it was his life's ambition to invent that something. He studied physics and became a professor at Clark University.

In 1926, almost thirty years after the idea first came to him, Robert Goddard was ready to try his experiment. On a farm in Auburn, just outside Worcester, he launched the world's first liquid-fueled rocket into the air. Goddard is remembered as the father of modern rocketry. His work made modern space flight possible. ■

Fruitlands Museum. Fruitlands includes the Shaker Museum, which commemorates another group of freethinkers who lived here from 1780 to 1918; the Indian Museum, which has Native American artifacts; and a gallery of landscape paintings.

A statue of a lamb on the common in Sterling commemorates the children's poem "Mary Had a Little Lamb." Sarah Josepha Hale composed it in the early 1800s, basing it on a local incident.

Connecticut Valley

Deerfield, in the northern part of the Connecticut Valley, is the home of Deerfield Academy (a private college preparatory school), established in 1797 and still in operation. Much of the town is like an open-air museum. Twenty-four houses were built before the American Revolution, and twenty-three others date from before 1850. Fourteen of these homes are open for guided tours. Historic Deerfield is one of the most beautiful and best preserved of New England's early settlements.

The campus of Smith College in Northampton

Springfield is the major industrial and cultural center of this region. Five leading colleges are located in the Connecticut Valley between Deerfield and Springfield—Amherst College, Hampshire College, the Amherst campus of the University of Massachusetts, Smith College, and Mount Holyoke College.

The Berkshires

Berkshire County is the state's playground for skiing in winter, hiking in summer, and other kinds of outdoor recreation. Summer in the Berkshires brings a wealth of entertainment, including classical and popular music, drama, and dance.

Williamstown, in the northern Berkshires, is the home of Williams College. This highly rated school was founded in 1793.

The Mohawk Trail, a 63-mile (101-km) scenic highway, stretches across northwestern Massachusetts from just west of Williamstown to the Connecticut River. It runs through the industrial town of North Adams, where there is a natural marble bridge. The feminist leader Susan B. Anthony was born in the neighboring town of Adams.

The largest city in the Berkshires is Pittsfield, an industrial and cultural center. The Hancock Shaker Village, a living-history museum, is there. Arrowhead, now a museum, was Herman Melville's Home while he was writing *Moby-Dick*.

Opposite: Hiking the Appalachian Trail through the Berkshires

CHAPTER SEVEN

A Glorious Covenant

The constitution of Massachusetts has stood the test of time. Called "a glorious covenant" when it was adopted, this document is the world's oldest written constitution still in use.

A committee of the legislature wrote a first draft in 1777 and presented it to the town meetings for a vote. Because it did not contain a bill of rights, the voters rejected it. A second version, written mostly by John Adams and complete with a declaration of rights, was accepted by the voters, ratified, and formally adopted on June 16, 1780. Only Massachusetts and New Hampshire gave voters a chance to accept or reject the state constitution at town meetings.

The official name of this state is the Commonwealth of Massachusetts. Three other states, Virginia, Pennsylvania, and Kentucky, are also officially named "commonwealths." The word comes from the old English *commonweal,* meaning "the common welfare." It appealed to John Adams and others because it suggests a government of the people—a democracy. There is no legal difference between the words "state" and "commonwealth," and both are commonly used.

All U.S. citizens eighteen years of age or older who are residents of Massachusetts are eligible to vote in state and national elections. The Massachusetts constitution provides for three branches of government: executive, legislative, and judicial.

Executive Branch

Massachusetts voters elect six people every two years to head the executive branch of government. As the chief administrator of the

Opposite: The Massachusetts statehouse

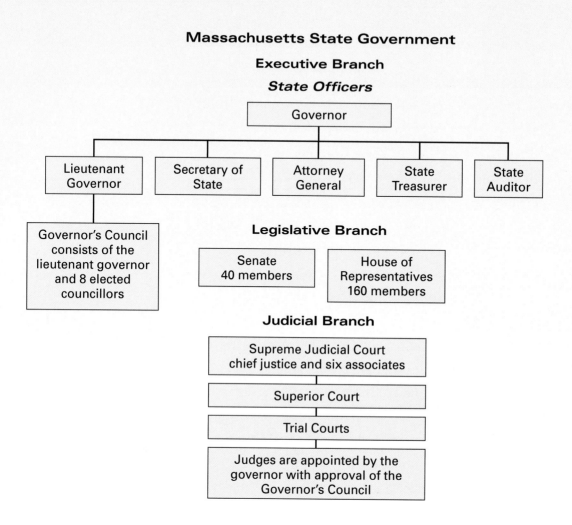

Massachusetts State Government

Executive Branch

State Officers

Governor

Lieutenant Governor | Secretary of State | Attorney General | State Treasurer | State Auditor

Governor's Council consists of the lieutenant governor and 8 elected councillors

Legislative Branch

Senate 40 members | House of Representatives 160 members

Judicial Branch

Supreme Judicial Court chief justice and six associates

Superior Court

Trial Courts

Judges are appointed by the governor with approval of the Governor's Council

state, the governor prepares the annual budget, nominates officers of the courts, and appoints most state department heads. All bills passed by the legislature are submitted to the governor for signature or veto. The governor appoints a secretary to head each of several executive departments.

The lieutenant governor serves as acting governor in case of the absence, death, or removal of the governor. The lieutenant gover-

Massachusetts Governors

Name	Party	Term			
John Hancock	None	1780–1785	Benjamin F. Butler	Dem.	1883-1884
James Bowdoin	None	1785–1787	George D. Robinson	Rep.	1884–1887
John Hancock	None	1787–1793	Oliver Ames	Rep.	1887–1890
Samuel Adams	None	1794–1797	John Q. A. Brackett	Rep.	1890–1891
Increase Sumner	Federalist	1797–1799	William E. Russell	Dem.	1891–1894
Caleb Strong	Federalist	1800–1807	Frederic T. Greenhalge	Rep.	1894–1896
James Sullivan	Dem.-Rep.	1807–1808	Roger Wolcott	Rep.	1896–1900
Levi Lincoln	Dem.-Rep.	1808–1809	Winthrop M. Crane	Rep.	1900–1903
Christopher Gore	Federalist	1809–1810	John L. Bates	Rep.	1903–1905
Elbridge Gerry	Dem.-Rep.	1810–1812	William L. Douglas	Dem.	1905–1906
Caleb Strong	Federalist	1812–1816	Curtis Guild, Jr.	Rep.	1906–1909
John Brooks	Federalist	1816–1823	Eben S. Draper	Rep.	1909–1911
William Eustis	Dem.-Rep.	1823–1825	Eugene N. Foss	Dem.	1911–1914
Marcus Morton	Dem.-Rep.	1825	David I. Walsh	Dem.	1914–1916
Levi Lincoln	Dem.-Rep.	1825–1834	Samuel W. McCall	Rep.	1916–1919
John Davis	Whig	1834–1835	Calvin Coolidge	Rep.	1919–1921
Samuel Armstrong	Whig	1835–1836	Channing H. Cox	Rep.	1921–1925
Edward Everett	Whig	1836–1840	Alvin T. Fuller	Rep.	1925–1929
Marcus Morton	Dem.	1840–1841	Frank G. Allen	Rep.	1929–1931
John Davis	Whig	1841–1843	Joseph B. Ely	Dem.	1931–1935
Marcus Morton	Dem.	1843–1844	James M. Curley	Dem.	1935–1937
George N. Briggs	Whig	1844–1851	Charles F. Hurley	Dem.	1937–1939
George S. Boutwell	Dem.	1851–1853	Leverett Saltonstall	Rep.	1939–1945
John H. Clifford	Whig	1853–1854	Maurice J. Tobin	Dem.	1945–1947
Emory Washburn	Whig	1854–1855	Robert F. Bradford	Rep.	1947–1949
Henry J. Gardner	Know Nothing	1855–1858	Paul A. Dever	Dem.	1949–1953
			Christian A. Herter	Rep.	1953–1957
Nathaniel P. Banks	Rep.	1858–1861	Foster Furcolo	Dem.	1957–1961
John A. Andrew	Rep.	1861–1866	John A. Volpe	Rep.	1961–1963
Alexander H. Bullock	Rep.	1866–1869	Endicott Peabody	Dem.	1963–1965
William Claflin	Rep.	1869–1872	John A. Volpe	Rep.	1965–1969
William B. Washburn	Rep.	1872–1874	Francis W. Sargent	Rep.	1969–1975
Thomas Talbot	Rep.	1874–1875	Michael S. Dukakis	Dem.	1975–1979
William Gaston	Dem.	1875–1876	Edward J. King	Dem.	1979–1983
Alexander H. Rice	Rep.	1876–1879	Michael S. Dukakis	Dem.	1983–1991
Thomas Talbot	Rep.	1879–1880	William F. Weld	Rep.	1991–1997
John D. Long	Rep.	1880–1883	Paul Cellucci	Rep.	1997–

Paul Cellucci became acting governor in 1997 after William Weld resigned when he was nominated to be Ambassador to Mexico.

nor and eight councillors make up the executive council. The councillors represent districts and are elected for two-year terms. The council certifies election results and has the power to approve judicial appointments and pardons and to authorize expenditures from the state treasury.

The secretary of state is in charge of state records, administers elections, and is responsible for the preservation of historic sites.

The attorney general serves as the lawyer for the commonwealth in all court proceedings. Consumer and environmental protection are also the responsibility of the attorney general.

The treasurer/receiver-general is custodian of all state funds and authorizes payments from these funds. The state board of retirement and state lottery commission are under the treasurer's jurisdiction.

The state auditor must audit all state accounts at least every two years.

John Hancock, First Governor of the Commonwealth

Have you every heard someone say, "Put your John Hancock there"? This slang expression, meaning "sign this," is more than 200 years old.

John Hancock, a wealthy Boston merchant, was one of the founders of our nation. He presided over the Continental Congress from 1775 to 1777 and was the first to sign the Declaration of Independence on July 4, 1776. He wrote his name large because, it was said, he wanted to be sure the king of England wouldn't need glasses to read it. It was an imposing signature on this nation's most important document. So, before long, people began to use his name as a synonym for the word *signature*.

John Hancock was also a member of the convention that adopted the Massachusetts constitution. In 1780, he was elected the first governor of the state. ■

Legislative Branch

The Massachusetts legislature is officially named the General Court. There are two houses: a 40-member senate and a 160-member house of representatives. Members of the legislature are elected for two-year terms.

Any citizen of Massachusetts may file a bill through a legislator. This is called the right of free petition. Most bills originate from senate or house members, however.

Once a bill is filed, it is given to a committee for study and for public hearings. The committee then brings it to the house or senate with a recommendation either to pass it into law or reject it. Both sides must agree on the wording of a bill before it can become a law.

When they have agreed, the bill is sent to the governor, who can do one of four things: sign it into law, return it to the legislature with a suggested amendment, veto it, or just refuse to sign it. If a law is vetoed, the legislature can override the veto by a two-thirds vote in both houses. If the governor refuses to sign the bills, it becomes law without the signature after ten days—unless the legislature adjourns before the ten days are up. That instance is called a pocket veto, and the bill dies.

Judicial Branch

The governor appoints judges to the Massachusetts courts. They hold their jobs until they reach the age of seventy. The Supreme Judicial Court of Massachusetts is made up of a chief justice and six associate justices. This court advises the governor and the legislature on questions of law.

The New England Town Meeting

Early each spring in most New England towns, voters come together to make decisions about their local government. This cherished tradition goes back to colonial days.

In an open town meeting, any voter can express opinions about anything concerning the town. There may be a debate, followed by a vote, on whether or not to build a new school. One person may complain about how long it takes to get the roads plowed after a blizzard, while another argues that the budget for snow removal is already too high. The old-fashioned New England town meeting is grassroots democracy in action.

Civil and criminal cases are held in divisions of a unified trial court. Its highest department is the superior court, which has a chief justice and sixty-six associate justices. Other departments are the district, housing, juvenile, land, and probate courts.

Local Government

County government in Massachusetts varies from county to county. Some changes are currently under consideration, but at present, county government has limited power in Massachusetts.

Massachusetts cities are governed by mayors and city councils. Towns usually have a governing body called a board of selectmen. The members are usually elected to serve for one or two years.

Massachusetts counties

State Seal and State Flag

The state seal is the oldest symbol of Massachusetts. It was adopted by Governor John Hancock in 1780 and made official by the General Court in 1885. It is circular, with Latin words that mean "Seal of the Republic of Massachusetts" around the outer edge. Inside is a coat of arms—a blue shield with a five-pointed star and the figure of a Native American holding a bow in one hand and an arrow in the other. The arrow is pointed downward, to signify peace, and the star symbolizes Massachusetts as one of the original thirteen states. A Latin motto is written in gold on a blue ribbon around the bottom of the shield. *Ense petit placidam sub libertate quietem* means "By the sword we seek peace but peace only under liberty."

The present form of the state flag, adopted in 1971, has the coat of arms on a field of white on both sides of the flag. ◼

The State Song
"All Hail to Massachusetts"
Words and Music by Arthur J. Marsh

All hail to Massachusetts, the land of the free and the brave!
For Bunker Hill and Charlestown, and flag we love to wave
For Lexington and Concord, and the shot heard round the world;
All hail to Massachusetts, we'll keep her flag unfurled.
She stands upright for freedom's light that shines from sea to sea;
All hail to Massachusetts! Our country 'tis of thee.

All hail to grand old Bay State, the home of the bean and the cod,
Where Pilgrims found a landing and gave their thanks to God.
A land of opportunity in the good old U.S.A.
Where men live long and prosper, and people come to stay.
Don't sell her short but learn to court her industry and stride;
All hail to grand old Bay State! The land of Pilgrims' pride!

All hail to Massachusetts, renowned in the Hall of Fame!
How proudly wave her banners emblazoned with her name!
In unity and brotherhood, sons and daughters go hand in hand;
All hail to Massachusetts, there is no finer land!
It's M-A-S-S-A-C-H-U-S-E-T-T-S.
All hail to Massachusetts! All hail! All hail! All hail! ◼

Massachusetts State Symbols

Massachusetts has—at last count—thirty official state symbols. Except for the state seal, most have been designated by the General Court in this century, about half of them since 1980.

State flower: Mayflower This small pink or white wildflower grows best in evergreen woods and in sandy or rocky soil. It is also known as trailing arbutus and ground laurel. Appearing in early spring, it has five petals and a pleasant fragrance. It was adopted by the General Court as an official emblem on May 1, 1918. Unfortunately, it has become quite rare and is now listed as endangered.

State tree: American elm Each autumn, the green leaves of this large shade tree (top, left) change to bright yellow. In the past, it was one of the most common and easily identified trees in eastern North America, but too many elms have died of Dutch elm disease. This symbol commemorates an elm on Cambridge Common, marking the spot where General George Washington took command of the Continental army in 1775.

State bird: Chickadee Also called titmouse, tomtit, and dick-

eybird, the chickadee (bottom, left) is easily identified by its cheerful call: "chick-adee-dee-dee." It has gray, black, and light brown markings and white cheeks. Its long tail makes up about half its length of only 4 to 5 inches (10 to 13 cm).

State beverage: Cranberry juice In tribute to the huge cranberry crop produced by Massachusetts each year, this drink was named the official beverage of the commonwealth in 1970.

State fish: Cod Native Americans and Massachusetts colonists used codfish for food and fertilizer.

State marine mammal: Whale Whales were important to the economy of the early Massachusetts colonists. They were hunted so much they almost became extinct. At present the population is slowly rebuilding, and whale-watching excursions have taken the place of whale hunting.

State insect: Ladybug A second-grade class selected the ladybug (opposite, top) as the state insect. These little bugs are red or yellow with black, red, white, or yellow spots. They help gardeners and farmers because they eat aphids, scale insects, and other plant pests.

State muffin: Corn muffin
Because it has been a basic element in the diet of Northeasterners since colonial days, schoolchildren asked the legislature in 1986 to make the corn muffin an official state emblem. The request was granted.

State folk song: "Massachusetts" This song by Arlo Guthrie was named the official folk song of the commonwealth in 1981.

State heroine: Deborah Sampson Deborah Sampson (bottom, right) joined the Continental army to fight in the American Revolution. She disguised herself as a man and enlisted as Robert Shurtleff. Her gender was discovered when she was wounded in battle. After the war, she traveled and gave speeches about her experiences. She was awarded a military pension, the first ever given to a woman. The governor proclaimed May 23 as a day to remember her enlistment. In 1983, more than 200 years after the Revolution, the legislature recognized her officially as a state heroine.

State historic rock: Plymouth Rock The legislature commemorated another historic event, the landing of the Pilgrims at Plymouth, by naming Plymouth Rock the official state rock. Although the Pilgrims did not actually land on the rock, it remains a historical symbol.

State gem: Rhodonite Varying in color from a light pink to deep rose or reddish pink, rhondonite is the most beautiful gem found in the state.

State mineral: Babingtonite Massachusetts is one of the few places where babingtonite, a lustrous jet-black mineral, is found.

CHAPTER EIGHT

Making a Living

English colonists in the New World were hardworking people. They got to work immediately to build their settlements. Feeding themselves and their families was a top priority. They hunted and fished, dug for clams, and caught lobsters. They traded for furs with the Native Americans. They cut down trees and planted crops. It did not take them long to produce enough for their own needs, with some left over for trading.

The Bounty of the Sea

By far the most profitable natural resource in New England came from the sea. People had been sailing across the ocean to find the huge schools of fish along the North Atlantic coast long before colonists came to stay. Atlantic fish, especially cod and mackerel, could be salted down and taken to faraway ports for sale. Boston soon became a major commercial center.

A crab fisher with his catch

Shipbuilding was an important industry from the very earliest days. The forests were full of tall, straight trees that provided excellent lumber for ships. Whaling was another profitable occupation. Sailors searched the waters, looking for the great sperm whales that swam up and down the Atlantic coasts. Many whale products were used to make everyday things such as candles, lamp oil, and soap. Whalebone was carved into handles for whips and other objects. Some 360 whaling ships were sailing from Nan-

Opposite: A cranberry bog on Nantucket

The Sacred Cod and Holy Mackerel

A 5-foot (1.5-m) wooden carving known as the Sacred Cod hangs in the statehouse in Boston.

Fishing is the oldest industry in Massachusetts, and the codfish has been an unofficial state symbol since colonial days. The first carved fish hung over the colonial legislature while it was in session. The original carving was destroyed by fire in 1747; a second met its doom during the Revolution.

The current emblem was carved in 1784. It has been with the Massachusetts House of Representatives ever since, except for a brief period in 1933 when Harvard University students "cod-napped" it.

The state legislature made the cod the official fish of Massachusetts in 1974. Another wooden fish hangs in the senate chamber. This one is known as the Holy Mackerel. ▪

tucket, New Bedford, and Marblehead by the time of the American Revolution.

Whaling became an obsolete occupation when oil was discovered in Pennsylvania. Almost overnight, people turned from whale oil to kerosene for lighting.

Textiles

Shipping and trading with faraway places increased after the Revolution, but the War of 1812 interfered seriously with those enterprises. However, while maritime trade was declining, the industrial age was beginning in Massachusetts.

In this 1912 photograph, women check woolen textiles before they are shipped.

It all started with Francis Cabot Lowell's cotton mills in Boston. Lowell, Lawrence, Chicopee, Fall River, and New Bedford rapidly became centers for textile manufacture. Lawrence was a center for wool processing, and Boston was the nation's center for trade in woolen cloth. For about 100 years, textile manufacturing was the most important industry in Massachusetts. Shoe manufacture, carried on in Lynn, Brockton, and Haverhill, was second.

Machines break down, wear out, and need improvements, so another industry developed to take care of the needs of the textile and shoe manufacturers. Factories were built in Boston, Springfield, and Worcester to make machinery and machine tools.

Beginning in the 1920s, textile and shoe manufacturers began leaving New England and moving south for cheaper labor. The exodus was nearly complete by the 1950s.

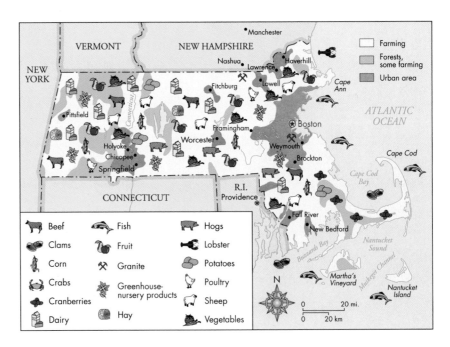

Massachusetts natural resources

What Massachusetts Grows, Manufactures, and Mines

Agriculture and Fishing	Manufacturing	Mining
Greenhouse and nursery products	Scientific instruments	Sand and gravel
Cranberries	Electrical equipment	Crushed stone
Milk	Machinery	
Flounder	Printing equipment	
Scallops		

Manufacturing Today

Recent years have seen big changes in Massachusetts industry. The electronics revolution of the late twentieth century brought new companies to the state. The many prominent colleges and universities, especially in the Boston metropolitan area, furnished a pool of talent for research in science-related fields.

The major products manufactured in Massachusetts today are scientific instruments, electrical and electronic equipment, machinery (including computers), and printing equipment. About 5 percent of the employees in manufacturing are in the textile and shoe

Circuit-board assembly in a state-of-the-art manufacturing plant

A Game Manufacturer

The oldest and largest company manufacturing games for children and adults started in Springfield, Massachusetts, in 1860. You have probably played several Milton Bradley games. Some of the currently popular ones are Twister®, Stratego®, Scategories®, Piction- ary®, Jurrasic Park Game®, Electronic Battleship®, and Scrabble®.

It all started with a board game called the Checkered Game of Life, invented by a printer named Milton Bradley. The company still bears his name and is still in Massachusetts. ■

industries. Other manufactured products include processed foods, paper and paper products, tools, and plastics.

Highway 128, which loops around the Boston area from Braintree to Gloucester, has been called the Golden Semicircle because many high-tech companies are located there. The route goes through Essex and Middlesex, two counties that lead the state in

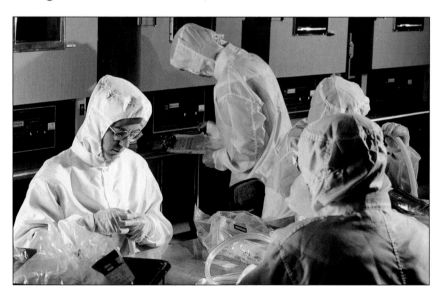

High-technology industries are prevalent along Highway 128.

Edwin Land

Not everything was at a standstill during the Great Depression. A new company opened in Boston in 1937 to manufacture lenses. Edwin Land, Polaroid's founder and brilliant inventor, secured 537 U.S. patents on his inventions, more than any other person except Thomas Edison.

In 1947, Land produced the first instant-picture camera. This invention boosted the Polaroid Corporation to a billion-dollar company employing 18,000 people. Land was a genius, more an inventor than a businessman. His company made a lot of money for many years, but that was not his primary interest. He used to scoff at the profit motive for business. He is supposed to have said, "The bottom line is in heaven."

electrical and electronic equipment manufacture. Recently, there has been some changeover from computer hardware to software development and bioresearch.

Manufacturing employs 17 percent of the state's workforce. Transportation, communications, and utilities use 4 percent, construction, 3 percent, and agriculture and fishing, 1 percent.

Service Industries

Employment in recent years has increased in education, medicine, finance, government, and trade. Massachusetts cities have diversified—they no longer depend on a single industry as they once did.

About 31 of every 100 employed people in Massachusetts work in a service field such as health care, education, law, computer programming, and engineering. Massachusetts General Hospital is

Bioresearch is an important industry in Massachusetts.

one of the world's leading centers of medical research.

Other service industries employ about 44 percent of the workforce. These include wholesale and retail trade, government, finance, insurance, and real estate. Boston is a major financial center, with two of the country's largest banks headquartered there. Other large financial firms are based in Springfield and Worcester.

Agriculture

The thin and rocky soil that covers much of Massachusetts cannot compete with the great farmlands of the Midwest in production. Only 14 percent of the state is farmland, and the farms are small and specialized, averaging a little under 100 acres (40.5 ha). Farmers concentrate on products that have a high cash value.

Nursery and greenhouse products—mostly flowers and ornamental shrubs—produce one-fourth of the state's farm income. Cranberries are the second most important crop. About half of all

A Cranberry Tour

If cranberries are a part of your Thanksgiving dinner, thank the Native Americans who introduced them to the Pilgrims. The Wampanoag people mixed the bright red berries with venison to make a dish called pemmican. The Pilgrims ate cranberries raw or cooked them with maple syrup. The town of Carver, named for the first governor of Plymouth Colony, is the leading producer of the fruit.

Cranberries grow on vines in bogs—wet, spongy soil. At the Cranberry Harvest Festival on Columbus Day weekend each fall, visitors watch the colorful process of gathering the fruit.

First, the bogs are flooded with water and then a kind of giant eggbeater churns up the water. As the berries fall off the vines, they float to the top of the water, where they are gathered for processing (above). The festival is held at the Edaville Cranberry Bogs, off Route 58 in South Carver.

Cranberry World Visitors' Center on the Plymouth waterfront has exhibits on the history of cranberries from precolonial days to the present, how they are grown and harvested, and various methods of preparing them. ▪

the cranberries grown in the United States come from the coastal lowlands in eastern Massachusetts. Many Americans consider this fruit a necessary part of a Thanksgiving dinner.

Other farm products include tobacco, apples, and dairy products. Most of the dairy farms are in the eastern part of the Connecticut Valley.

Other Industries

Although fishing makes up only 1 percent of the state's economy, Massachusetts is a leading commercial fishing state, and New Bedford, Gloucester, and Boston are among the foremost fishing ports in the nation. Clams, crabs, squid, and other seafood are also plentiful.

Fishing enjoyed prosperous times at the beginning of the twentieth century when fast transportation made it possible to ship fresh fish for long distances. The development of techniques for the quick freezing of fish also helped the industry. More recently, overfishing in the North Atlantic has hurt the fishing business. High operating costs and increased imports of fish and seafood are additional handicaps.

Millions of international travelers fly in and out of Boston, which is closer to western Europe than any other major U.S. city. Logan International Airport in East Boston is one of the nation's busiest airports.

Tourism, both domestic and international, draws people to the state. The most popular destinations are Boston, Cape Cod, and the Berkshires.

Opposite: An aerial view of Logan International Airport in Boston

CHAPTER NINE

Who Are the Bay Staters?

I f you were to meet half a dozen young people from a school in Boston or Worcester, they might include: a boy whose ancestors have lived in Massachusetts ever since 1620; another whose Irish forebears have been in the state for 150 years; a girl whose French-Canadian grandparents came here from Quebec and who has lots of cousins in Canada; a girl whose mother is a Wampanoag from Martha's Vineyard and whose father is a Menominee from Wisconsin; a dark-skinned boy whose ancestors came here from the Cape Verdean Islands in the 1600s and were never slaves; a girl, born in Puerto Rico, who will inform you she's an American citizen by birth, as are all Puerto Ricans.

Today's Massachusetts citizens come in many colors and speak with many accents. They are descended from people of many lands. It wasn't always so. For some 170 years after the first Europeans settled in Massachusetts, the population was homogeneous, or similar. At least 82 percent of the people were English-born or of English ancestry, and another 8 percent were Scots or Irish.

By 1790, only a few Native Americans remained; many had died of various causes. African-Americans made up about 2 percent of the total. The first ones had arrived in Massachusetts in 1638.

Adults and kids alike cool off in the Christian Science Center's reflecting pool.

Opposite: An Armenian family bakery in Watertown

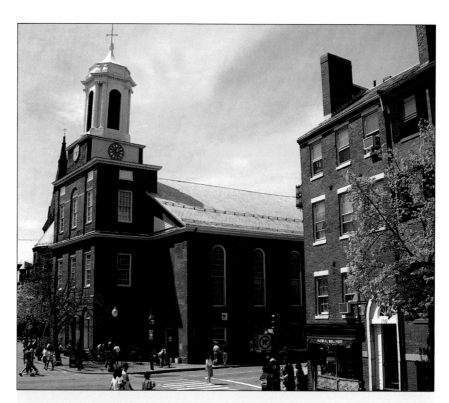

African-American Heritage

Several landmarks in the greater Boston area commemorate the history of the African-Americans who have lived there since colonial times. The Black Heritage trail starts at the African Meeting House on Beacon Hill. The meetinghouse, a part of the Museum of Afro-American History, was built in 1806. The New England Anti-Slavery Society was founded there in 1832. The museum has a large collection of papers, crafts, and arts.

The 54th Regiment Memorial and the Boston Massacre Monument, both on Boston Common, tell of the involvement of African-Americans in the American Revolution and the Civil War. The African-American Heritage Trail in Cambridge includes the home of William Wells Brown, the nation's first African-American novelist, and the house where educator and writer W. E. B. DuBois lived while earning the first Harvard University doctorate granted to an African-American. ■

Some were indentured servants; some worked on the docks, on ships, or in construction.

In 1790, the young U.S. government decided to take a census of the nation's population. The people in each state were counted, and certain information about them, such as their ethnic background and where they were born, was noted. Almost 500,000 people lived in the state, including the counties now in Maine that were then part of Massachusetts. About 12 percent of the U.S. population lived in Massachusetts.

A census has been taken every ten years since then. Census figures give us a great deal of useful information. The 1990 census reported more than 6 million people in Massachusetts.

Immigration

The first big wave of immigration to Massachusetts started in the 1840s. Most of the newcomers came from Ireland. Living conditions were desperate in that country—1 million people had died of starvation during a severe potato famine, and another million had left their mother country for other lands. By 1860, more than half the residents in Boston were Irish.

The elite of Massachusetts—those who ran the government and major businesses—were known as the Boston Brahmins. They were all white Anglo-Saxon Protestants, and thought of Boston as their city, giving it nicknames that illustrated their pride in it. They

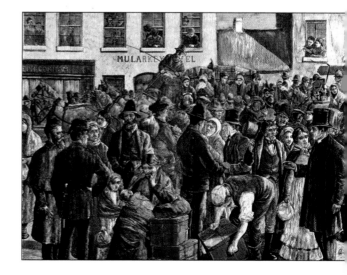

Irish emigrants preparing to leave from county Galway during the potato famine (1845–1849)

The Life of a Mill Girl

In 1835, Harriet Hanson went to work in the cotton mills (above) of Lowell when she was ten years old. Her father had died six years after she was born. Her mother struggled to take care of Harriet and the other three children, but it was difficult. They had barely enough to eat and were often cold.

Harriet's aunt Angeline persuaded the family to move from Boston to Lowell, where women were needed to run boardinghouses. Harriet helped her mother care for forty male boarders, plus her own family, but she wanted to do more. She begged her mother to let her get a job in a mill, and her mother agreed.

The work was not terribly hard at first, according to Harriet. She was one of the doffers, who were all little girls. Their job was to remove full bobbins (spools of thread) from the spinning machines and replace them with empty ones. They ran with their boxes of bobbins, making the exchange as quickly as possible, so the machines would not be idle.

Their actual work took only about fifteen minutes of each hour. The rest of the time they read, knitted, or played games. The workday began at 5:00 A.M. and ended at 7:00 P.M., with a half hour off for breakfast and midday dinner; they were paid two dollars a week.

Education was still very important, and a law required the mill owners to give children under fourteen three months off per year to attend school. Harriet and her friends were great readers. They read about the working conditions of English factory children, who were treated badly and even whipped. "We thought of ourselves as well off, in our cozy corner of the mill," she wrote, "enjoying ourselves in our own way, with our good mothers and our warm suppers awaiting us when the going-out bell should ring."

Harriet worked in the mills until she was twenty-three. Fifty years later, she published a book about her experiences: *Loom and Spindle, or Life among the Early Mill Girls.*

Lowell, the largest manufacturing center in the United States at that time, was a completely planned industrial city. The company recruited young women from New England farms to work in the mills. Housing was provided in supervised boardinghouses.

The young ladies were encouraged to use their spare time for self-improvement. Libraries and educational lectures were sponsored. The "Lowell factory system" became famous.

For a few years, the factory girls had a pretty good time. Most of them stayed in the mills for a limited time. Working conditions got much worse as the years went by. Many workers who came later developed terrible lung diseases, caused by years of breathing dust and lint in the mills.

In her book, Harriet Hanson Robinson regrets the passing of "the lost Eden which I have tried to describe." ■

called it the Cradle of Liberty, the Athens of America, and even the Hub of the Universe.

The Yankees did not welcome the Irish with open arms. There was a great deal of religious prejudice between Protestant Yankees and the Roman Catholic Irish. Job discrimination was glaring and offensive. Signs on some company doors said, "No Irish need apply." But through hard work and perseverance, plus the force of their numbers, the Irish soon gained power in Boston politics. The first Irish-born mayor was elected in 1885.

Thousands of newly freed slaves flocked to Massachusetts after the Civil War. In 1900, the state had five times as many African-Americans as in 1865.

As manufacturing became more important in Massachusetts, hundreds of thousands of immigrants came to the state to find work. They came from Italy, Poland, Russia, Greece, Portugal, Slovakia, Germany, Scandinavia, and Canada. The state's population grew about 20 percent every ten years until 1910.

In the 1900s, the rate of population growth slowed, but the ethnic background of newcomers became even more diverse. Today, many immigrants come

Boston's North End is home to many Italian stores and restaurants.

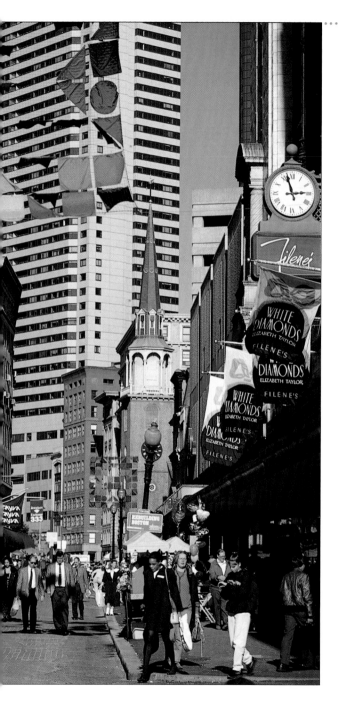

The lively, crowded
city-center of Boston

from the Caribbean: Cuba, Haiti, the Dominican Republic, and Puerto Rico. Others are from Korea, Vietnam, and Middle Eastern countries.

Boston has always been famous for its baked beans. Some people compare the mix of people in Massachusetts to a bean pot. Each ethnic group can be singled out, like individual beans, but it takes the combination to create a tasty dish. The mixture of cultures, languages, histories, and facial features in Massachusetts is rich and fascinating.

Where They Live

Massachusetts is one of the most densely populated states in the nation. It ranks thirteenth among the states in population and forty-fifth in area. Most recent immigrants and their families live in urban areas. The western, more rural, part of the state has a greater proportion of people whose ancestors were the original colonists.

In the 1970s, some Massachusetts cities declined in population. This was the period of "urban flight," when many residents and businesses moved to the suburbs, a trend that seems to have slowed.

Boston Baked Beans

Ingredients:

    1 pound dried navy beans
    1 tablespoon salt
    1/2 pound salt pork
    1 tablespoon dry mustard
    1/3 cup dark brown sugar (maple sugar, if possible)
    1/3 cup molasses

Directions:

Wash the beans and soak them overnight in 1 quart of water.

Preheat oven to 300°F.
Drain the beans and save the water.
Bring the water to a boil in a saucepan.
Meanwhile, cut off 1/3 of the salt pork and remove the rind. Cut the rindless salt pork into small, 1/2 inch cubes. Take the remaining 2/3 of the salt pork and cut it into 4 wide strips. Place the cubes of salt pork into a bean pot. Put the beans on top of the pork.

When the water in the saucepan is boiling, add the salt, mustard, brown or maple sugar, and molasses. Mix well and simmer for 1 to 2 minutes. Then pour the mixture over the beans. Place the strips of salt pork over the beans and cover the pot.

Bake for about 6 hours, checking every hour or so and adding water when necessary. During the final hour, uncover the pot.

Before serving, remove the strips of salt pork and stir the beans. Add more salt, mustard, or sugar to taste.

Serve with hot brown bread.

Serves 6 to 10.

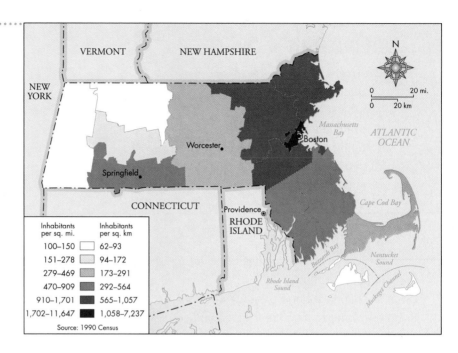

Massachusetts population density

Religion

In the seventeenth century, the Massachusetts Puritans founded the Congregational Church. There was no distinction between church law and civil law. The church leaders made the rules, and everyone had to obey them whether or not they were members of the Congregational Church. No other churches were allowed before 1690, and the state officially supported the Congregational Church until 1834. This type of government is called a *theocracy*.

The Irish immigrants were overwhelmingly Roman Catholic. So were the French Canadians, the Italians, and many other immigrants. Today, more Catholics than Protestants live in Massachusetts.

Language

The 1990 census reported that about 15 percent of the people in Massachusetts spoke languages other than English at home. These

Population of Massachusetts Cities (1990)

Boston	574,283
Worcester	169,759
Springfield	156,983
Lowell	103,439
New Bedford	99,922
Cambridge	95,802

languages include Spanish, Portuguese, French, Italian, Chinese, Polish, Greek, German, Korean, Vietnamese, and Arabic.

The public schools face great challenges. Bilingual programs, especially for Spanish-speaking students, have been initiated in some cities.

Education

The Massachusetts colonists valued education and lost no time in setting up schools. Within their first ten years, they founded the Boston Latin School and Harvard College. School laws were passed in 1642 and 1647 that required towns to provide education for all children.

Schools in Massachusetts educate children from many cultures.

Harvard's main purpose was to prepare students for the ministry. One requirement for a bachelor's degree was the ability to translate the Bible into Latin.

Two centuries later, during the reform years of the mid-nineteenth century, laws were passed to ensure that public schools would be available for all children. And, in sharp contrast to the Puritan days, religious teaching in public schools was discouraged.

Samuel Phillips Hall, Phillips Academy, in Andover

A prestigious private school, Phillips Academy in Andover, has been in operation since 1778. The nation's first college for women, Mount Holyoke, was founded in South Hadley in 1837. Among the early graduates were some of the nation's first women doctors.

Mount Holyoke is one of a group of highly respected private women's colleges, all of them in the Northeast, known as the Seven Sisters Colleges. (However, since some of these schools are now coed, this term is seldom used). Four of these schools are in Massachusetts. In addition to Mount Holyoke, the others are Wellesley College in Wellesley, founded in 1870; Smith College in Northampton, the largest private liberal-arts college for women in

The Boston Accent

Outsiders love to imitate the Boston accent. "Bostonese" leaves out the letter "r" in some words and adds an "r" at the end of other words. For example, "Harvard" becomes *Hah-v'd.* A "harbor" is *hah-buh;* a "bar" is a *bah.* "Park" is *pahk;* in fact, it is almost, but not quite, *pack.*

In some words, the "r" be-comes an extra syllable: "here" sounds like *he-ah,* "there" is *they-ah.*

But on the other hand, the word "saw" takes on an added "r" in Bostonese: *sawr.* And Bostonians end their prayers by saying *Arr-men* (Amen). The letter "o" may be flattened out or ignored, as in Boston, pronounced *Bah-st'n.* ∎

the United States, founded in 1876; and Radcliffe College in Cambridge, founded in 1879.

Boston has one of the heaviest concentrations of educational institutions anywhere. About fifty colleges and universities are located within 20 miles (32 km) of the statehouse. The population of greater Boston increases by about 250,000 when students start the new semester each fall.

Massachusetts Institute of Technology (MIT) in Cambridge, one of the nation's leading research institutions, dates from 1861. Many breakthroughs in science and technology are the result of work done at MIT.

In the little town of Woods Hole, on Cape Cod, two unusual research and educational facilities are devoted to the study of everything about the sea. The Woods Hole Marine Biological Laboratory was founded in 1888 to study marine life. The Woods Hole Oceanographic Institution, opened in 1930, studies and grants graduate degrees in all aspects of marine sciences.

CHAPTER TEN

Enjoying Leisure Time

Name your sport, and you can find a place to enjoy it in Massachusetts. The ocean and its beaches are perfect for sailing, sunbathing, swimming, beachcombing, and digging for clams. Rowing, canoeing, and kayaking are popular on the rivers and lakes. You'll find campgrounds and biking and hiking trails all around the state. The Appalachian Trail, a hiking path that extends from Maine to Georgia, runs through the Berkshires. The Berkshires are also popular with mountain bikers and climbers. And facilities for ice skaters, sledders, and skiers are close to wherever you are in Massachusetts.

The Swan Boats on Boston Common have provided passengers a few minutes of perfect relaxation for more than 100 years. The boats are shaped like swans, complete with head and wings. A captain pedals the boat, while the passengers sit on benches for a brief glide over the pond.

The Swan Boats on Boston Common

Opposite: Kayaking at Zoar Gap on the Deerfield River

For longer rides, take a sightseeing cruise in Boston Harbor or at other points along the shore. Whale-watching cruises during the migrating season are offered from several ports.

Spectator Sports

Nearly every sports enthusiast in New England feels a deep loyalty to the four professional teams based in Massachusetts. They root for the Boston Red Sox in baseball, the Boston Celtics in basketball, the New England Patriots in football, and the Boston Bruins in hockey.

The first World Series in baseball was held in 1903, and the Boston Pilgrims won—five games to three. Four years later, the Pilgrims changed their name to the Red Sox. They won four World Series between 1912 and 1918, but Boston's demise began soon after, when the Red Sox owner sold one of his pitchers to the rival New York Yankees. That pitcher quickly turned into the most amazing hitter ever—Babe Ruth—and he single-handedly made the Yankees into the greatest dynasty in sports. The Red Sox, meanwhile, were devastated.

In the 1930s, Boston was blessed with a new legend, Ted Williams, who today is renowned as the greatest Red Sox player of all time and one of the best hitters ever to pick up a bat. The "Splendid Splinter" (he was skinny as a young player) hit 521 home runs and earned a lifetime batting average of .344. But despite his heroics, he could never lead the Red Sox past the rival Yankees. In fact, the Red Sox have not won a World Series since their 1918 championship—the longest dry spell in the American League.

Ted Williams in 1952

Fenway Park and the Garden

Bay Staters love little Fenway Park, the smallest major-league ballpark in the United States, although it was among the largest when it was built in 1912. Cozy, intimate, and old-fashioned, it still has a hand-operated scoreboard, live organ music, and real grass. A 37-foot (11.3-m) wall in left field is known as the Green Monster. A fly ball that goes over the top becomes the shortest home run in any baseball park. Playing defense in left field at Fenway Park is the toughest outfield job because each fly ball might bounce off the Monster in a different way.

Equally loved was the old Boston Garden, where the Boston Celtics and Bruins played for many decades. The Celtics played basketball on an old, wooden, parquet floor (made up of squares of wood). When the Bruins played a hockey game, the floor was taken apart, revealing an ice rink underneath. Dozens of championship banners hung in the rafters of the Garden, giving it a unique aura of history and achievement. But it all came to an end in 1995, when the Celtics and Bruins moved to Boston's new Fleet Center, and the Garden was destroyed. Many New Englanders shed tears after seeing their fabled sports palace in ruins. ▪

Opposite: The Boston Celtics playing the New Jersey Nets at the Fleet Center in Boston

Since the earliest days of the National Hockey League, the Boston Bruins have been one of the top teams, winning the championship Stanley Cup five times. In recent times, however, the Bruins have experienced lean years. Their last era of true dominance was the 1970s, when the great Bobby Orr led the team to the Stanley Cup twice—in 1970 and 1972.

The Boston Celtics are even more legendary than the Bruins. In fact, many sports fans argue that the Celtics are the greatest sports franchise of all time. Led by coach Red Auerbach and the Hall-of-Fame center Bill Russell, the Celtics won an incredible eleven NBA championships in thirteen years from 1957 to 1969. The Celtics then faded—but only slightly, winning five more championships before 1986. Larry Bird led the team through the 1980s, and his deadly accurate

shooting and heroic leadership solidified his place as a New England sports legend.

The game of basketball originated in Springfield, Massachusetts, in 1891. James Naismith, a physical education teacher at the YMCA Training School (now Springfield College), was its inventor. He borrowed ideas from lacrosse, soccer, and other sports of the day. His aim was to create a game that would be good for both physical exercise and mental concentration and that could be played year-round indoors. The new game caught on immediately and was soon being played by both men and women.

Exhibits about the history of basketball, video highlights of outstanding games, and tributes to the great players of the game are on display at Naismith Memorial Basketball Hall of Fame in Springfield. Visitors are challenged to test their own shooting skills while standing on a moving sidewalk.

Performing Arts in the Berkshires

Imagine a Friday night in July. The air is warm, and there's a pleasant light breeze. The sky is filled with twinkling stars. You've come to listen to an outdoor concert at Tanglewood, an estate just outside Lenox in the Berkshires.

Every one of the 6,000 seats in the Music Shed, a structure designed by the famous architect Eero Saarinen, is occupied. You and your family have decided to sit on the lawn, so you've brought along a picnic dinner and folding chairs.

Tanglewood is the summer home of the Boston Symphony Orchestra. The sound of music echoes in the Berkshire Hills from late June through August each year. The Boston Pops Orchestra and

other jazz and popular musicians also appear in concert during the summer festival.

Tanglewood is one of the best-known summer arts festivals in the northeastern United States, but it is only one of many in the Berkshires. Other music festivals and summer programs are presented in Lee, Sheffield, Great Barrington, Pittsfield, and Lenox.

Picnickers enjoy classical music on the lawn at Tanglewood.

Jacob's Pillow Dance Festival, in Lee, has been hosting performances by leading dance companies for more than fifty years. Pittsfield has a professional ballet company.

Outstanding theater is another longtime tradition in the Berkshires. The Williamstown Theatre Festival, Miniature Theatre of Chester, and Berkshire Theatre Festival in Stockbridge present stage productions throughout the summer months. The nationally known Shakespeare & Company, in Lenox, performs from May to December.

The Athens of America

Boston has been a cultural center since its very early days, featuring concerts, plays, and ballets. Colleges and universities, as well as professional companies, have extensive calendars of performances.

Cultural activities are also geared to the interests of children. The Boston Symphony Orchestra presents one-hour performances for elementary schoolchildren in fall and spring. Musicians demonstrate various instruments.

Popular with families are the Arts in the Parks—concerts and programs presented on the banks of the Charles River. Puppet shows are staged year-round at the Puppet Showplace in Brookline. Puppet performances are also presented during July and August at the Toy Cupboard Theatre in South Lancaster.

The Children's Theatre in Watertown features about 100 children aged 5 to 15 acting and singing in musicals. They also go on tour to schools for the deaf, where the dialogue and lyrics are interpreted in sign language.

Museums and Libraries

Dozens of top-notch museums, libraries, and historic sites are found in and around Boston. The aristocratic and wealthy members of early Boston society appreciated the arts and education, and they founded many institutions that have survived for two centuries or more.

A Fourth of July concert at the Hatch Shell on the Charles River

Boston is the largest and oldest cultural center in Massachusetts, but it is one among many. Towns throughout the state have established public institutions that reflect the Yankee appreciation of the finer things of life. Every town has a public library, and most have historical museums. Art museums, beautiful parks, and college campuses are nearly as plentiful.

Old North Church

Probably the most famous building in Boston is Christ Church, popularly known as the Old North Church, or just Old North. This was where the lantern was hung to signal Paul Revere and William Dawes that they should mount their horses and warn people that the British were about to attack.

Henry Wadsworth Longfellow's poem, "Paul Revere's Ride," told the story:

Listen, my children, and you shall hear
Of the midnight ride of Paul Revere,
On the eighteenth of April, in Seventy-five;
Hardly a man is now alive
Who remembers that famous day and year . . .

One, if by land, and two, if by sea;
And I on the opposite shore will be,
Ready to ride and spread the alarm,
Through every Middlesex village and farm . . .

Old North, a Georgian-style brick building with tall windows, was built in 1723, fifty-two years before the lantern was hung in its lofty steeple. It has been in continuous use as a house of worship ever since. The church has tall box pews, an organ decorated with cherubs, and two brass chandeliers, each topped by a dove of peace. A replica of one of the famous 1775 signal lanterns hangs in a window. ■

Two Boston Painters

John Singleton Copley, who was born in Boston in 1738 and died in 1815, was America's first great portrait painter. His portraits of Paul Revere, John Hancock, and other prominent people of the Colonial period hang in the Museum of Fine Arts in Boston. He spent his later years in London, where he turned to religious and historical subjects for his paintings.

A self-portrait of John Singleton Copley

Charles Bulfinch

A few years after the end of the American Revolution, a twenty-four-year-old Bostonian presented a plan for a new statehouse to the state legislature. While the legislators were thinking it over, young Charles Bulfinch designed the Connecticut statehouse and was earning a reputation for his work.

Finally, after eight years of debate, Massachusetts legislators told Bulfinch to go ahead.

In 1798, Bulfinch led a ceremonial procession up Beacon Street from the old statehouse to the stately new one he had designed. His creation still dominates the Boston scene from the top of Beacon Hill.

Charles Bulfinch was the first full-time architect in the United States. A few years later he completed the U.S. Capitol in Washington, D.C. ■

Another very successful portrait painter, John Singer Sargent, lived a century after Copley. He studied in Paris and worked with the French artist Claude Monet. At the height of his career, in the 1890s, he returned to Boston. He did much of the decorative painting in the Museum of Fine Arts. Other Sargent paintings can be seen in the Isabella Stewart Gardner Museum, Symphony Hall, Boston Athenaeum, and Boston Public Library.

Literature

Massachusetts played a starring role in American history during two different periods. Before and during the American Revolution, sons and daughters of Massachusetts were in the forefront of political leadership. Then, during the middle of the nineteenth century, a period of outstanding literary and intellectual activity brought Massachusetts leaders into the limelight again.

The Literary Crowd

The Alcott family lived for a time in Concord, where they were close friends of Ralph Waldo Emerson. Bronson Alcott was a transcendentalist and a teacher. His daughter, Louisa May Alcott, wrote magazine stories and novels for young people. Many of her books, such as *Little Women* and *Little Men,* are still very popular. Several movies have been based on *Little Women.*

Another neighbor and friend was nature essayist Henry David Thoreau.

During the same period, Nathaniel Hawthorne was in Salem, writing novels based on New England life. Both Hawthorne and Herman Melville used fiction to illustrate society's flaws.

Massachusetts poets John Greenleaf Whittier and Henry Wadsworth Longfellow also took their themes from reality, folklore, and history. Longfellow was the most popular poet of his time. James Russell Lowell was a prominent poet, satirist, essayist, editor, and college teacher. Emily Dickinson, a shy, reclusive woman, wrote beautiful poetry, though most of it was not published until after her death.

Horatio Alger was a native son of Massachusetts but lived in New York. He wrote more than 100 books for boys, all on the theme of "rags to riches." ■

The cover of Horatio Alger's book *Ragged Dick*

So many authors, poets, teachers, lecturers, and other intellectual leaders were clustered in the same region at the same time that the period has been called the Flowering of New England. Many of them lived in Concord and Boston, some in western Massachusetts. Ralph Waldo Emerson, known as the Sage of Concord, was at the center of this creative explosion. He knew and encouraged all the others.

Some of these people were part of a philosophical movement called transcendentalism. They questioned the conservative religious beliefs of the time and supported such reforms as educational innovation, abolitionism, and feminism.

For more than 450 years, Massachusetts men and women have been among the nation's leaders. Self-government, education, manufacturing, literature, philosophy, environmentalism, abolition of slavery, women's rights, rocket science, electronics, medicine, the arts—all have been influenced by people from this state.

Henry Wadsworth Longfellow wrote in praise of democracy and hope for its future. As Massachusetts and the nation move into the next millennium, these words, written more than 100 years ago, still seem appropriate:

> . . . *Sail on, O Ship of State!*
> *Sail on, O Union, strong and great!*
> *Humanity with all its fears*
> *With all the hopes of future years,*
> *Is hanging breathless on thy fate!*

Timeline

United States History

Massachusetts State History

	1498 John Cabot, an English explorer, sails along the Massachusetts coast.
1607 The first permanent British settlement is established in North America at Jamestown.	
1620 Pilgrims found Plymouth Colony, the second permanent British settlement.	**1620** Pilgrims settle at Plymouth.
	1630 Puritans establish the Massachusetts Bay Colony near present-day Boston.
	1635 Harvard becomes the first college in the colonies.
	1692 Hundreds of people are accused of witchcraft at Salem.
	1770 Colonists are killed during the Boston Massacre.
	1773 Bostonians protest British taxation by dumping crates of tea in the harbor.
1776 America declares its independence from England.	**1775** The American Revolution begins with battles at Lexington and Concord.
1783 The Treaty of Paris officially ends the Revolutionary War in America.	**1780** Massachusetts adopts a state constitution.
1787 The U.S. Constitution is written.	
1803 The Louisiana Purchase almost doubles the size of the United States.	**1788** Massachusetts becomes the sixth state.
1812–15 The United States and Britain fight the War of 1812.	
	1820 Maine is separated from Massachusetts and becomes a state.
	1843 Dorothea Dix initiates prison reform.
1861–65 The North and South fight each other in the American Civil War.	**1861** Massachusetts troops are the first to die in the American Civil War.

United States History

The United States is **1917-18** involved in World War I.

The stock market crashes, **1929** plunging the United States into the Great Depression.

The United States fights in **1941-45** World War II.

The United States becomes a **1945** charter member of the United Nations.

The United States fights **1951-53** in the Korean War.

The U.S. Congress enacts a series of **1964** groundbreaking civil rights laws.

The United States **1964-73** engages in the Vietnam War.

The United States and other **1991** nations fight the brief Persian Gulf War against Iraq.

Massachusetts State History

1890 Stephen M. Babcock develops a machine to test the amount of butterfat in milk, boosting dairy production.

1912 Textile mill workers strike for higher wages.

1919 Governor Calvin Coolidge settles a Boston police strike and rises to national prominence.

1958 Massachusetts citizens elect both a Democratic governor and legislature for the first time.

1960 Senator John F. Kennedy is elected president of the United States.

1971 Massachusetts begins major restructuring of its state government.

1974 A federal court orders the integration of Boston public schools.

1997 Governor William Weld resigns in an unsuccessful attempt to attain U.S. Senate approval of his nomination to be ambassador to Mexico.

Fast Facts

Massachusetts state
capitol

Chickadee

Statehood date February 6, 1788, the 6th state

Origin of state name Named for the Massachuset people, who lived in the region when the Pilgrims arrived.

State capital Boston

State nickname Bay State, Old Colony State

State motto *Ense petit placidam sub libertate quietem* (By the sword we seek peace but peace only under liberty).

State bird Chickadee

State flower Mayflower (trailing arbutus)

State fish Cod

State gem Rhodonite

State song "All Hail to Massachusetts"

State tree American elm

State mineral Babingtonite

State insect Ladybug

State horse Morgan horse

Cape Cod

The Connecticut River

Massachusetts school-children

State fair	Springfield (September)
Total area; rank	9,241 sq. mi. (23,934 sq km); 45th
Land; rank	7,838 sq. mi. (20,300 sq km); 45th
Water; rank	1,403 sq. mi. (3,634 sq km); 21st
Inland water; **rank**	424 sq. mi. (1,098 sq km); 35th
Coastal water; **rank**	979 sq. mi. (2,536 sq km); 7th
Geographic center	Worcester
Latitude and longitude	Massachusetts is located approximately between 41° 14' and 42° 53' N and 73° 30' and 70° 5' W
Highest point	Mount Greylock, 3,491 feet (1,064 m)
Lowest point	Sea level along Atlantic coast
Largest city	Boston
Number of counties	14
Longest river	Connecticut River, 66 miles (106 km)
Population; rank	6,029,051 (1990 census); 13th
Density	730 persons per sq. mi. (282 per sq km)
Population distribution	84% urban, 16% rural

Ethnic distribution (does not equal 100%)		
White		89.84%
African-American		4.99%
Hispanic		4.78%
Asian and Pacific Islanders		2.38%
Other		2.58%
Native American		0.20%

Winter in
Massachusetts

**Record high
temperature** 107°F (42°C) at New Bedford and Chester on
August 2, 1975

**Record low
temperature** –34°F (–37°C) at Birch Hill Dam on January
18, 1957

**Average July
temperature** 71°F (22°C)

**Average January
temperature** 25°F (–4°C)

**Average yearly
precipitation** 45 inches (114 cm)

Massachusetts Natural Areas

National Seashore

Cape Cod National Seashore comprises 43,569 acres (17,633 ha) of
shoreline. It includes a number of historic buildings.

National Historic Sites

The National Park Service maintains thirteen sites in Massachusetts,
including:

Adams Historic Site, the home of the Adams family, including Presidents John Adams and John Quincy Adams.

Boston African American Historic Site, fifteen pre–Civil War structures
relating to the history of Boston's black community, and the African
Meeting House, the oldest standing black church in the United States.

John Fitzgerald Kennedy National Historic Site (Brookline), the birth-place of the thirty-fifth president.

Henry Wadsworth Longfellow National Historic Site (Cambridge),
which celebrates Longfellow's work while at Harvard.

Great Point Lighthouse,
Nantucket

Walden Pond

Minute Man Historical Park (Lexington and Concord), which preserves the site of the battle that launched the American Revolution.

Salem Maritime Historic Site, which includes Derby Wharf and other buildings from the era of shipping to East Asia.

State Parks and Forests
Massachusetts has ninety-seven state parks, including Walden Pond, Skinner State Park, and Nickerson State Park on Cape Cod. The largest state forest is October Mountain State Forest with more than 16,000 acres (6,475 ha). Since the 1800s, forestland has almost tripled.

Sports Teams

The Boston Celtics

NCAA Teams (Division 1)
Boston College Eagles

Boston University Terriers

Harvard University Crimson

College of the Holy Cross Crusaders

Northeastern University Huskies

University of Massachusetts–Amherst Minutemen

Major League Baseball
Boston Red Sox

National Basketball Association
Boston Celtics

National Football League
New England Patriots

National Hockey League
Boston Bruins

Cultural Institutions

Libraries

The Harvard University Library (Cambridge) was the first library established in the American colonies. It is the largest university library in the United States.

Athenaeum (Boston) contains George Washington's collection of books.

John F. Kennedy Library (Boston) contains the papers of the former president.

Boston Public Library is the largest public library in the state.

Museums

Museum of Fine Arts (Boston) has the finest collection of Asian art in the world.

Isabella Stewart Gardner Museum (Boston) has many outstanding Renaissance paintings.

George Walter Vincent Smith Art Museum (Springfield), *Worcester Art Museum*, and *Sterling and Francine Clark Art Institute* (Williamstown) are among the nation's best-known smaller museums.

The Hatch Shell in Boston

Performing Arts

Massachusetts has four major opera companies, two major symphony orchestras, one major dance company, and two professional theater companies.

Universities and Colleges

In the mid-1990s, Massachusetts had 31 public and 86 private institutions of higher learning.

Smith College in Northampton

Annual Events

January–March

Bay State Games in Williamstown and North Adams (last week in February)

New England Spring Flower Show in Boston (March)

Spring Bulb Show in Northampton (March)

April–June

Daffodil Festival on Nantucket Island (April)

Whale-watch Cruises from Cape Ann to Cape Cod (April–October)

Hanging of lanterns in the steeple of the Old North Church in Boston (third Sunday in April)

Boston Marathon (third Monday in April)

Cambridge River Festival (May)

Antique Automobile Show in Stockbridge (Sunday of Memorial Day weekend)

Cape Cod Chowder Festival in Hyannis (June)

Williamstown Theatre Festival (June–August)

Bunker Hill Day in Charlestown (June 17)

Tanglewood Music Festival in Lenox (mid-June–August)

Blessing of Fishing Fleets in Gloucester and Provincetown (late June)

July–September

Esplanade Concerts in Boston (July)

Up-Country Hot-Air Balloon Fair in Greenfield (July)

Harborfest in Boston (July)

Jacob's Pillow Dance Festival in Becket (July–August)

Pilgrim's Progress Processional in Plymouth (Fridays, July–August)

Sandcastle Contest in Nantucket (August)

The Stanley Steamer

Gloucester

Harvesting cranberries

Teddy Bear Rally in Amherst (August)

The "Big E" State Fair in West Springfield (September)

World Kielbasa Festival in Chicopee (weekend after Labor Day)

Cranberry Harvest Festival in Harwich (weekend after Labor Day)

Apple/Peach Festival in Acushnet (second weekend in September)

October–December

Scallop Festival in Buzzards Bay (October)

Rowing Regatta on the Charles River in Boston and Cambridge (October)

Haunted Happenings in Salem (October)

Pilgrim's Progress Processional and Pilgrim Thanksgiving Day in Plymouth (Thanksgiving Day)

Ralph Waldo Emerson

Benjamin Franklin

Famous People

John Adams (1735–1826)	President of the United States
John Quincy Adams (1767–1848)	President of the United States
Samuel Adams (1722–1803)	Patriot
Louisa May Alcott (1832–1888)	Author
Susan B. Anthony (1820–1906)	Social reformer
Crispus Attucks (1723?–1770)	Patriot
Clara Barton (1821–1912)	Founder of the American Red Cross
William Bradford (1590–1657)	Governor of Plymouth Colony
William Cullen Bryant (1794–1878)	Poet and editor
Luther Burbank (1849–1926)	Horticulturalist
Bette Davis (1908–1989)	Actor
Emily Dickinson (1830–1886)	Poet

Henry David Thoreau

Ralph Waldo Emerson (1803–1882)	Poet and essayist
Benjamin Franklin (1706–1790)	Statesman, businessman, scientist, diplomat, publisher
William Lloyd Garrison (1805–1879)	Journalist and reformer
Robert Goddard (1882–1945)	Rocket scientist
John Hancock (1737–1793)	Statesman
Nathaniel Hawthorne (1804–1864)	Author
Oliver Wendell Holmes (1841–1935)	Jurist
Winslow Homer (1836–1910)	Painter
Elias Howe (1819–1867)	Inventor
Anne Hutchinson (1591–1643)	Puritan leader
John F. Kennedy (1917–1963)	President of the United States
Robert F. Kennedy (1925–1968)	Politician
Henry Wadsworth Longfellow (1817–1882)	Poet
Francis Cabot Lowell (1775–1817)	Textile manufacturer
Samuel Morse (1791–1872)	Artist and inventor
George Peabody (1795–1869)	Merchant and philanthropist
Edgar Allan Poe (1809–1849)	Writer
Paul Revere (1735–1818)	Silversmith and patriot
Henry David Thoreau (1817–1862)	Philosopher and naturalist
Daniel Webster (1782–1852)	Orator
Eli Whitney (1765–1825)	Inventor
John Greenleaf Whittier (1807–1892)	Poet
Ted Williams (1918–)	Baseball player

To Find Out More

History

- Cherry, Lynne. *A River Ran Wild*. San Diego: Harcourt, 1992.

- Cox, Clinton. *Undying Glory*. New York: Scholastic, 1991.

- Fradin, Dennis B. *Massachusetts*. Chicago: Childrens Press, 1991.

- Monke, Ingrid. *Boston*. New York: Dillon Press, 1988.

- San Souci, Robert. *Wyeth's Pilgrims*. San Francisco: Chronicle, 1991.

- Waters, Kate. *Sarah Morton's Day: A Day in the Life of a Pilgrim Girl*. New York: Scholastic, 1989.

Biographies

- Anderson, Madelyn Klein. *Edgar Allan Poe: A Mystery*. New York: Franklin Watts, 1993.

- Ilgenfritz, Elizabeth. *Anne Hutchinson*. New York: Chelsea House, 1990.

- Kent, Zachary. *John F. Kennedy*. Chicago: Childrens Press, 1989.

Fiction

- Fritz, Jean. *And Then What Happened, Paul Revere?* New York: Coward, McCann & Geoghegan, 1973.

- Fritz, Jean. *Why Don't You Get a Horse, Sam Adams?* New York: Coward, McCann & Geoghegan, 1974.

Lawson, Robert. *Ben and Me: A New and Astonishing Life of Benjamin Franklin as Written by his Good Mouse Amos.* Boston: Little Brown, 1939.

Websites

Massachusetts Map of World Wide Web Resources
http://donald.phast.umass. edu/misc/mass.html
Clickable maps lead to additional resources about universities, science research sites, cities and towns, and annual events.

Massachusetts Vacation Information
http://www.mass-vacation.com
Extensive list of vacation destinations as well as a calendar of events.

Commonwealth of Massachusetts—MAGNet
http://www.state.ma.us/
Links to state government agencies, 351 local communities, and many reference sources about the state

Addresses

Office of Travel and Tourism
100 Cambridge Street
13th floor
Boston, MA 02202
For information about travel in Massachusetts

Office of Business Development
1 Ashburton Place
21st floor
Boston, MA 02108
For information about the economy of Massachusetts

Office of the Secretary of State
Citizen Information Service
1 Ashburton Place
Room 1611
Boston, MA 02108
For information about the government and history of Massachusetts

Index

Page numbers in *italics* indicate illustrations.

Meet the Author

Sylvia McNair was born in Korea and believes she inherited a love of travel from her missionary parents. She grew up in Vermont, traveled often to Massachusetts, and lived for a summer in Boston. After graduating from Oberlin College, she held a variety of jobs, married, had four children, and settled in the Chicago area. She now lives in Evanston, Illinois. She is the author of several travel guides and more than a dozen books for young people published by Children's Press.

"The first step to writing any book is to read. I always head for my local libraries and consult several encyclopedias and other reference books. Then I look for other books of fiction or nonfiction that are related to the history, geography, or people of the place I'm working on. I use my computer to search for information on the Internet.

"If I'm working on a book about a state, I make a trip to the capital of that state as soon as possible. Usually I find a great deal of good information in the state library that isn't easily available anywhere else. Then I arrange to borrow some of the materials through the interlibrary loan service. I look in that city's bookstores, and I usually end up buying several books for my personal library.

"Last (although I've been working on it all along) comes the writing part. I sit at my computer for several hours each day. I use up reams of paper as I print out many drafts before I'm satisfied with the result.

"I learn so much while reading and writing, and there's nothing more fascinating than learning more about my own land."

McNair has traveled in all fifty states and more than forty countries. "I love to travel, but there's no region I love more than New England, my childhood home."

Photo Credits

Photographs ©:

A. Blake Gardner: 7 top center, 52, 54 top, 58, 60

Alex S. MacLean: 57, 97, 129 center

AllSport USA: 131 bottom (Jamie Squire), 115

AP/Wide World Photos: 50 (Susan Walsh), 6 bottom, 47, 113

Art Resource: 38 top, 121, 135, 59, (National Portrait Gallery, Washington D.C.), 56 inset

AT&T Laboratories: 39

Bill Miles: 94

Boston Globe Photo: 80

Clark University: 45

Corbis-Bettmann: 20, 30, 33, 42, 89, 102, 125, 134 bottom

Envision: 105 (Steven Needham)

Folio, Inc.: 65 (Claudia Dhimitri), 74, 132 bottom (Catherine Ursillo)

H. Armstrong Roberts, Inc.: 10 (J. Blank), 35 (R. Krubner), 8, 64 (F. Sieb), 67, 133 bottom (J. Urwiller)

John F. Kennedy Library: 46

Kindra Clineff: back cover, 6 top left, 7 top right, 9, 34 top, 54 bottom, 56, 68, 69, 71, 72, 75, 76, 86, 88, 92, 95, 98, 103, 107, 110, 111, 119, 128 top, 129 bottom, 131 top, 132 top, 134 top

Library of Congress: 19 top

MIT Museum: 44

Monkmeyer Press: 7 top left, 87 (Arlene Collins)

N.E. Stock Photo: 114 (Thomas H. Mitchell)

North Wind Picture Archives: 22, 24, 27, 29, 32, 36, 37, 80, 85 bottom, 101, 122

Phillips Academy Andover: 108

Photo Researchers: 7 bottom, 85 top (Tom Branch), 70, 130 bottom (Shea), 84 bottom, 128 bottom (James Zipp)

Polaroid Archives: 93

Stock Boston: 62, 130 top (Donald Dietz), 99 (Michael Dwyer), 15, 40 (Leonard Harris), 6 top center, 53, 129 top (Kent Knudson), 117 (Lincoln Russell), 100 (Eric A. Wessman)

Stock Montage, Inc.: 6 top right, 14, 16, 17, 18, 19 bottom, 21, 25, 26, 28, 31, 41, 133 top, 134 center

Sygma: 48 (Bob Gomel), 49 (Ira Wyman)

The Mount Holyoke College Archives and Special Collections: 43

Tony Stone Images: 104 (Gary Moon), 2, 34 bottom (Vito Palmisano), cover (Chuck Pefley), 12 (Steve Vidler)

UPI/Corbis-Bettmann: 51, 63, 73

Visuals Unlimited: 84 top (Mack Henly).

Maps by XNR Productions, Inc.